Supercouple Syndrome

Supercouple Syndrome

How Overworked Couples
Can Beat Stress Together

Wayne M. Sotile, Ph.D.

Mary O. Sotile, M.A.

New York • Chichester • Weinheim • Brisbane • Singapore • Toronto

Library of Congress Cataloging-in-Publication Data:
Sotile, Wayne M., 1951–
    Supercouple syndrome : how overworked couples can beat stress
together / by Wayne M. Sotile, Mary O. Sotile.
        p.   cm.
    Includes index.
    ISBN 0-471-19402-6 (alk. paper)
        1. Dual-career families—United States.   2. Work and family—
United States.   3. Marriage—United States.   4. Stress (Psychology)
I. Sotile, Mary O.   II. Title.
HQ536.S675   1998
646.7'8—dc21   97-18067
                                                                CIP

Printed in the United States of America

10 9 8 7 6 5 4 3 2 1

To our daughters, Rebecca and Julia,
For being sisters we admire,
for blessing our lives with your presence,
and for carrying on our family traditions as you blaze your own trails.
Giving you each other is the best thing we ever did.

Contents

Preface

We are the new superheroes: a generation of men and women facing unprecedented changes and lofty expectations for fulfillment in three major arenas—family, work, and self. We push and challenge each other to get it all: success, health, and happiness. Compared to prior generations, we expect more. But, in the wake of the downsizing trend of the last decade, we also struggle more.

A new work ethic is emerging; one which calls for us to maintain flexibility, expect transition, redefine success, fight the right fight—and try to maintain reasonable balance between work, family, and personal life.

But we seldom meet a couple who reports a comfortable balance across their collective roles. That today's couples have achieved such a balance has become the 1990's version of the Beaver Cleaver family myth. With fewer than 15 percent of American households blessed with the luxury of an at-home spouse, how can a comfortable balance of roles exist? In truth, it can't. In facing our combination of roles, we have normalized workweeks of 85 to 110 hours.

So, we don't live in balance—we live the Big Life. Our expanded expectations and multiple roles lead us to become superpeople with exceptional coping strategies that keep us going despite our abnormal levels of stress, fatigue, and tension. We become experts at managing our responsibilities, but we remain rather inept at keeping our relationships alive. Indeed, the crunch of our "ready, set, go" lifestyles is hurting us at home and at work. The stresses that come with the juggling act we are living lead us to cope in ways that hurt relationships. This is what we call Supercouple Syndrome.

Couples who suffer from Supercouple Syndrome apply the same hard-charging traits that make them successful in the business world (being in control, staying competitive, striving for perfection, moving at a fast pace) to their relationships. This tactic makes their relationships burdensome. When our personal relationships suffer, we lose our stress stamina. We then burn out and drop out, both at home and at work. Some are doomed to the three Ds: drained, downsized and divorced.

New Hope for Happily (Enough) Ever After

Our research suggests that a new set of realistic, optimistic possibilities exists for today's Dynamic Duos—couples who use their relationships as havens from outside demands, who create appropriate boundaries, take time out to have fun, and nurture their partners by noticing everyday accomplishments. Who are these couples? What makes them different from stressed-out couples? What are their secrets to carving out healthy relationships in a crazy world?

We've been focused on answering these questions for the past 20 years. Our work began at the Duke University Medical Center, continued at Wake Forest University's Bowman Gray School of Medicine, and culminated in our private practice of medical psychology and marital/family therapy. We have personally counseled over 5,000 couples. Thousands more have attended our workshops and lectures. Collectively, we have had the privilege of spending nearly 60,000 hours with high-powered people who used their resources to create success in their work and in their personal lives.

The culmination of this research and counseling is the *BE*ating *S*tress *T*ogether (BEST) Program, designed to help today's chronically crazed, superachieving couples. The BEST program shows you how to follow nine easy steps to change your relationship style; by applying BEST, even the most stressed-out supercouples can become Dynamic Duos.

The case examples throughout this book are drawn from our clinical experiences. Descriptions and incidental facts have been altered to protect the confidentiality of our clients.

Acknowledgments

Our sincere thanks to the many people who made our own juggling act work as smoothly and pleasantly as it did while we wrote this book:

Kathy Hall, our assistant and office manager—for your daily acts of heroism on our behalf.

Lynn Swaim, our typist—for making Tuesday our favorite day, still after all these years.

Joyce Waters, our secretary—for so smoothly joining our motley crew.

Richard Martin, Elin Call, Lani Seltzer, Carol Walsh, and Cleaver Hillman, our colleagues—for being such pleasant and competent partners in practice.

Gail Ross, our literary agent—for your warmth, competence, and guidance.

The nice folks at North Market Street Graphics—for a great job, done on time!

The dynamic team at John Wiley & Sons—for believing in our concepts and for partnering with us to create a book we like.

Special thanks to Tracey Thornblade—for your astute editing.

And to Kelly Franklin, senior editor at John Wiley & Sons—for the enthusiasm, passion, and guidance that sculpted our manuscript into a book that we are proud of. Your tact and warmth made this our most pleasant publishing experience. We appreciate you.

To the thousands of courageous people who have allowed us the privilege of working with you at crucial junctions in your own journeys.

Finally, thanks to our families—the Sotiles, Milanoes, Owens, and Letts—for teaching us the values of family, hard work, and good fun; and for your generosity and graciousness.

Chapter One
_____

Two Incomes, No Sex

The trappings differ, but today's superachieving couples all have similar problems.

The Victims: Karen and John

Karen sat on our couch, crying as she recited a litany of confusion about yet another failed romance. "It seems that my relationships all end within three years. The guy makes the proverbial 'I just need a little space' announcement, and I *know* the end just began.

"I tried as hard as I could with John. I don't understand why it didn't last. I guess the fact that I have two kids was more of a problem for him than I knew.

"But I'll tell you this: I know that I'll survive. I survived my divorce. I've survived my dad's death and my mother's moving in for six months and now living six blocks from me. I've survived living on about 40 percent as much money as I used to. I'll survive this, too."

In a separate counseling session, John clarified: "As far as I'm concerned, the fact that Karen has two kids is a plus, not a problem. I love her kids.

"The problem is Karen; she's like a split personality. In some ways, she's the most generous person I know. She's always going out of her way to help others. But she is also the most competitive person I have ever met, and that's a real turn-off for me. She's competitive in a deceptive way. I mean, behind closed doors the woman acts like her life is a contest with everyone she has ever known. All she talks about is the flaws of her friends and relatives. And her stress is always the worst stress; her schedule is always the most hectic; her burdens are always the heaviest. It's a strange competition.

"Things were great for us during the first two years. But these past two years have been hell. I've tried to talk with her about this, but our talks end up sounding like a competition about who is less competitive. I'm fed up."

The Strugglers: Bruce and Marsha Malcom

The Malcoms were married as they were zooming up their respective career ladders. Bruce had just made partner in his law firm, and Marsha was one step away from taking over her family's real estate business. By the time their second child was born eight years later, they truly seemed to be thriving. They enjoyed a collective yearly income of $385,000. They showed mutual respect for each other's success and cooperated in orchestrating their 50-to-75-hour workweeks while sharing the responsibilities of parenting and running their home.

But beneath the surface things weren't so glowing. When they entered counseling, they had not had sex in over 18 months, ostensibly due to Marsha's mysterious loss of libido. "I don't know what happened," Bruce lamented. "We used to be such a hot couple. Given how lousy sex had been in each of our first marriages, passion was one of the big attractions for us. I don't know what in the hell is wrong with you!"

Marsha's response dripped with sarcasm. "I don't know, Bruce. Maybe what's wrong with me is that I'm tired of your telling me how I am supposed to live, spend money, drive, associate with my family, parent our kids, and respond to you in bed. You are *the* most controlling person I've ever been around."

Marsha had an endless list of complaints about Bruce. When she was driving, he offered helpful hints about which lanes of traffic would likely move the fastest. He also had the annoying habit of interrupting her during conversations. He finished Marsha's sentences, seemingly in an effort to move the conversation along and get to the point. He seemed unable to focus on one thing at a time. As he visited with his family over breakfast, he also reviewed his day's schedule while glancing at the newspaper and listening to the morning stock report.

Bruce responded to his wife's criticisms with his own searing observations. "Let's not pretend here. You aren't exactly Miss Mellow. You're never satisfied being where you are, no matter where you are. When you're home, you worry about the office. When you're at work, you agonize over what's happening at home. Yes, maybe I am a little controlling; maybe I do a lot of things at once; I admit it. But at least I'm available. You are gone most of the time. You pretend that you only work 45 hours per week, but, in truth, you never play! Between your work at work and your work at home—some of which, I swear, we could hire out—you are working your life and our marriage away."

The Thrivers: Mike and Belle Milano

It was traumatic when, after six years of stellar performance as an investment banker, Mike was told that he no longer had a job. Downsizing led to outsourcing his department's functions, and he found himself out of work for the first time in his achievement-filled life. And it happened during his wife's self-imposed hiatus from her own career. Four years prior, Belle had decided to put her marketing career on hold to be an at-home mom to their infant son.

Faced with an uncertain financial future, the Milanos weighed their options. First, they considered scaling down their lifestyle. Maybe they should sell their relatively new house. But they rejected that notion. This was their home; the place where they wanted to raise their family. They committed themselves to keeping it. They discussed the possibility of Belle's returning to work, but decided to delay that move until their son entered first grade. They held steady in their faith that Mike would find new work. But they didn't anticipate that the job search would take the 14 months that it did. Nor did they anticipate Belle's second pregnancy and the health problems it caused. After three months of bed rest, she miscarried.

By the time Mike joined a private investment firm, the Milanos had depleted their savings and had borrowed $20,000 from their parents. But they remained upbeat: "We faced this in the only way that made sense to us. I'm proud of Belle; she's a trooper who never stops fighting. I'm just sad about the baby and about the financial bind we are now in. Once I get solidly going in this new job, we'll try again to get pregnant. The money? Well, making money is my job. I've got a great opportunity with this new firm, and I plan to jump on it."

More than second-guessing their financial or family future, Belle worried about the effect that this career setback would have on Mike. She described her husband as a workaholic who had trouble controlling his temper: "Mike has always believed that he succeeds only because he works harder than everyone around him. He has so little faith in his natural talents and abilities. He can't relax if he has work to do, and of course, there's always work to do.

"This is not the first time we've been through something like this. Mike started his last job six years ago, after some horrible years caused by the fact that he hated his prior job and stayed angry all the time. I'm afraid about what this will do to him . . . and to us. Sometimes it's hard for me. I get tired of Mike's being so preoccupied and grouchy. So often, he's home, but he's not really relaxed.

"But, you know, I believe he does the best that he can. He's a good father, and he loves me with devotion. Plus, we still have more than our share of fun, at least compared to most couples I know. Thank God we committed ourselves to keeping our Tuesday-night-is-play-night rule sacred. We started that right before he quit his last job. We had it out then. He was working over 90 hours a week and was angry all the time. I told Mike then that I wouldn't stay married to him if he got lost in his workaholism and anger. And I refused to get pregnant until he did something about it. So he did.

"He vowed to me then that he would at least learn to create periods of recess from work and that he would look into making a career move. He kept his word; he made the move to the bank. He loved working there. Now this.

"But, I swear, I think those Tuesday night recesses from all of our worries and working keep us alive. I know that we'll make it; we've survived hard stuff before."

Who Are These People?

In different ways, these couples epitomize the new normal. They are *supercouples*—juggling multiple roles, managing complex families, and enduring incessant stress. In short, they are living the Big Life.

In adapting to the Big Life, we have become a society of exceptional copers, high-powered people who employ some combination of coping strategies that keep us going despite our abnormal levels of stress, fatigue, and tension. Stereotypical superachiever men and women hold down pressure-cooker jobs and exude an intimidating presence. But no matter what their occupations, if they endure and acclimate to ever increasing levels of stress, they're high powered.

Karen is surviving her divorce, single parenting, her father's death, her own multiple roles, and the end of a series of important romances.

Bruce and Marsha are juggling two demanding careers while parenting their two children and struggling with each other. Like many superachievers, they find it hard to find time for each other; and consequently, their romantic life has suffered. These end up being TINS couples—*Two Incomes, No Sex.*

Mike and Belle are battling the three Ds that plague so many couples today: They get *d*ownsized at work; *d*rained by their Big Life; and threatened with *d*ivorce. But the Milanos are winning this battle. Despite their financial strains, their career dramas, Mike's temper and workaholism, and their health scares and grief over Belle's miscarriage, they are trying to keep their love alive.

These stories depict most modern couples. We are a culture of stress-hardy copers. That's the good news. The bad news? Our methods for managing ourselves in the Big Life can kill our relationships.

Superachievers are able to do more, manage more, endure more, and achieve more than most people. They are able to deny themselves to get their work done—be it work at the office, the work of taking care of loved ones, or both. But when one or both partners lock into a superachiever coping style, they begin to suffer from

Supercouple Syndrome: The skills they use in managing their Big Life drain them of their tolerance, passion, and joy. Their relationships lose their zest; their families lose their warmth; and their creativity dwindles.

This book will teach you how to avoid the frustrations of Supercouple Syndrome. Instead of being part of a pair of stressed-out superachievers, you'll become part of a Dynamic Duo—mutually supportive, empowered, and committed to a good life together.

Chapter Two

Do You Suffer from Supercouple Syndrome?

Fully 70 percent of us evidence at least one high-powered coping habit that allows us to endure despite exceptional stress and strain. These coping strategies include:

- The ability to relentlessly work hard
- The tendency to control others
- Perfectionism
- Chronic hurry sickness—the tendency to rush, even when there is no objective need to do so
- The talent of doing and/or thinking more than one thing at once
- Burning competitiveness
- Stamina in facing the demands of home and work

In managing our Big Life, we develop the hallmark characteristic of exceptional copers: the capacity to go numb when stressed and keep on going. Because we have so much to do and feel it's important to get everything done, superachieving people easily become frustrated, irritable, and sometimes hostile and cynical. If you are living the Big Life, you probably spend considerable time preoccupied with your own anxieties, stresses, needs, and wants. This creates various forms of relationship narcissism—the tendency to be so preoccupied with the struggle to maintain personal control that we mismanage our relationships. For some, this shows up in the attitude, "Given how beaten-up I get from stress, I *deserve* to have my every need met, my every insecurity soothed, and my batteries recharged *by you*. You owe me! When you fail to deliver, I am free to unload my frustrations onto our relationship."

For others, relationship problems are caused by insensitivity to the people around them. Self-absorption and preoccupying anxiety come from living in a pressure-packed time crunch. Amid such stress, two things get ignored: the needs of others and the impact that our high-powered coping behaviors have on others. Here, relationship narcissism is fueled more by the sense that "I'm so anxious and burdened, I simply don't notice you or your needs."

Think of it in this way: If you're driving down the road at a leisurely pace—say 30 or 40 miles an hour—you are likely to be reasonably courteous to your passengers. You might tune into their conversations. You might ask, "Are you comfortable? Hot? Cold? Would you like to listen to the radio?"

But if you're driving 120 miles an hour, you won't care whether the other passengers are comfortable. You need to stay focused on the road ahead.

If you manage your life as a perpetual road race, there will be an inevitable toll on your relationships:

- If you are frequently exhausted from your superperson quests, you will drain the vibrancy out of your relationships.
- If you are controlling in your interactions, others will stop revealing themselves to you, fearing another unwanted invasion.
- If you are perfectionistic, your criticism will alienate others.
- If you are always in a rush—called *hurry sickness*—your connection with loved ones will be damaged.

- If you habitually do or think more than one thing at once, others will feel that you never fully attend to them.
- If you are excessively competitive, others will avoid spending time with you for fear of being put down.
- If you are impatient, others will feel anxious when around you.
- If you repeatedly show irritation and hostility, others will feel wounded, not nurtured, by you.

Are your coping styles hurting your relationship? Use the following exercise to answer this question.

SUPERACHIEVER SYNDROME SCALE

Instructions: Use the following scale to rate yourselves on each of the characteristics listed.

1	2	3	4	5
Never	*Sometimes*	*Often*	*Usually*	*Always*

	How often am I?	How often are you?
Time urgent	_____	_____
Impatient	_____	_____
Perfectionistic	_____	_____
Hostile/cynical	_____	_____
Controlling	_____	_____
Competitive	_____	_____
Involved in work	_____	_____
Hot-tempered	_____	_____
Irritable	_____	_____
Doing or thinking more than one thing at once.	_____	_____

This and other exercises in this book are intended to help you evaluate yourself and discover how you are similar to and different from other important people in your life. The point is to clarify how you might help each other become more effective emotional managers. We do *not* intend for you to use these exercises to label yourselves in negative ways.

As you look over your collective responses, take particular note of discrepancies between your self-ratings and the ways in which your partner perceives you. Most of us have somewhat inaccurate perspectives on the impact we have on others. Regardless of how positive our intentions may be, we do tend to get lost in our own coping hazes.

Give Me Control or Lose Me!

When faced with threats to their ability to control outcomes, superachievers kick into overdrive. In an urgent effort to regain control, they exaggerate their fail-safe survival strategies: The orderly become compulsive; the grouchy, hostile; the anxious panic; the hardworking go numb and get lost in workaholism.

If they fail to regain control—due to the limited influence they have on others, to circumstances beyond their control, or to their own limited abilities—many high-powered people drift into *vital exhaustion.* This strange form of passivity kills the comfortableness and closeness in their relationships. Vital exhaustion is accompanied by feelings of hopelessness and helplessness—feelings that are unfamiliar to most superachievers.

Vital exhaustion leads high-powered parents to seemingly give up struggling with adolescents they cannot control. It also leads couples to passively settle into their loss of romance and passion. An obvious consequence of corporate downsizing is vital exhaustion sapping the morale of high-powered employees in the workplace. A hidden consequence is vital exhaustion draining zest from the bedrooms of today's workers.

> Difficulty tolerating what goes on in relationships is the number one stressor for high-powered people.

Relationship issues are one of the areas that high-powered people neither fully control nor expertly handle. In large part this is because high-powered coping *creates* tension in relationships.

The Superachiever Paradox

Even if you're not particularly high powered when you begin a relationship, chances are you'll become so in reacting to your partners in the Big Life. This is because relationships organize around the most constant theme, and few things are as constant as the coping strategies we use in managing the stress epidemic we live in. The more stressed we become, the more high powered we get. But the more high powered we become, the more we struggle in relationships.

This happens because of a dangerous paradox. On one hand, high-powered people prove to be exceptions to many rules that apply to others. They endure more, cope better, and often accumulate and achieve more. But along the way, they develop a pocket of incompetence: managing relationships. Both at home and at work, they get lost in stress hazes and neglect or damage each other.

Relationship issues tend to be an awkward arena for hard-driving, competitive, time-urgent people, and superachievers don't like to delve into realms where they don't feel competent. Being chronically busy makes it easy to avoid dealing with others. Zooming in and out of contact, supercouples never settle down and attend to each other long enough to gain confidence and a sense of mastery in dealing with the complex emotions that fill intimate relationships.

Where Did the Intimacy Go?

Relationship intimacy can be measured in many ways:

- How often you interact affectionately
- How often you laugh at each other's jokes
- How often you say something nice to each other
- How often you compliment your partner in front of others
- How often you make love
- How often you are playful with each other
- How often you look each other in the eyes while conversing
- How often you give each other a little surprise
- How often you say "please" or "thank you" or "I'm sorry"

What happens to intimacy as a relationship unfolds? Most of us begin our romance in Bliss City, a place characterized by sky-high levels of intimacy. Here, aided by the intoxication and selective perceptions that come with the amphetamine-like love hormone called *phenylethylamine* (PEA), we each see what we need to see and be how we need to be to create harmony. We believe we have found in each other the fulfillment of all our dreams. We see in each other answers to our own unfulfilled potential, characteristics we each lack or feel awkward about. We fall in love with an intention of creating more wholeness in each other's life: I'm shy and you're outgoing; You're a workaholic, but I'm playful and nurturing; I'm hot-tempered, you're mellow. The two of us share the hope that we will join together and make one whole person, the bliss will continue, and the relationship will provide an island of refuge lasting a lifetime.

And we act as though this will, indeed, happen. We can't love each other enough! We even invent special ways of showing our love and affection. We concoct pet names for each other. We save silly but symbolic souvenirs of special events that we share. We bathe each other in attention and affection.

At the core of this early stage of romance is a relationship contract. Based on what we perceive and communicate, consciously and unconsciously, we assign to our mate and assume for ourselves a set of roles that create our particular relationship dance. The contract organizes us and defines for us who and how we will be as a couple, and our life together begins.

Then comes a stage we call *the little dipper.* We commit to each other, perhaps marry, and the tangible signs of intimacy dip. It's as though we reason, "Okay, Baby, it's time to get back to work now. Can't be doing this intimacy stuff all my life." As time goes on and our infatuation hormones dwindle, we discover that many of the traits we attributed to our partner simply aren't there. The landslide soon follows.

Typically between years 4 and 8, sometimes in tandem with the arrival of children, mortgages, unexpected setbacks, or otherwise exploding Big Lives, we lose each other. We feel double-crossed by this supposedly perfect partner. Those wonderful traits we saw in the other don't seem to be soothing our personal struggles. We are left with our workaholism, hot temper, shyness, or whatever we brought into this relationship.

What happens next tends to be tragic. During the disillusionment stage of their journey, most couples simply quit. Like Karen in our opening case vignettes, many go through a series of relatively brief relationships. Others, like Bruce and Marsha, settle into a "ready, set, go" lifestyle. Their days and weeks fill with stress, and their high-powered coping habits shape their relationship. As their vitality drains, their passion dwindles in tangible, measurable ways:

They stop playing, laughing, communicating, attending to, or even touching each other. They justify their malaise with rationalizations and with the unfortunately accurate observation that "this is the way most married couples live." They put aside romance and passion, settle for a functional relationship, and live semimiserably ever after. In short, they suffer from Supercouple Syndrome.

Are These Our Only Options?

Fortunately, an alternative exists. Certain couples learn to be Dynamic Duos, channeling their coping strengths and commitment to achievement toward keeping romance and intimacy alive. Dynamic Duos don't have fairy-tale marriages. No one remains in Bliss City for a lifetime. Because of the neurophysiology of love and romance, as a relationship ages, infatuation and PEA diminish. And as the Big Life gets bigger, the wear-and-tear effects of stress hurt any relationship. But Dynamic Duos learn to cooperate in order to handle their everyday stresses. As marriage and family therapists, we have had the privilege of being allowed private glimpses into the inner workings of thousands of couples who have had a lifetime romance. They, too, endured dips in intimacy and disillusionments.

But these couples did something else, something that set them apart from the pack. Like Mike and Belle Milano, they let the signs of struggling serve as a wake-up call in their relationships. They took responsibility for the effects that their lifestyles and their respective coping styles were having on their relationships. And they used their exceptional skills to change, not simply to endure. Even though the intensity of their connections diminished as they outgrew their infatuations, they learned to treat each other in ways that keep soothing endorphins flowing. These reformed superachievers become Dynamic Duos by applying a program aimed at *BE*ating *S*tress *T*ogether (BEST).

What Is Beating Stress Together?

BEST is about facing your stress demons while managing your personality-based coping patterns and personal stress reactions, all the while keeping an eye on your relationship dynamics. BESTers are the people who embrace positive attitudes, lifestyles, pleasures, and relationship dances. They take care to regularly disrupt problem coping and to cooperate with each other as they shape the situations, processes, and relationships that form the territory of their life together.

Let's elaborate this last point. One key to BEST is cooperating with your partners to create a fenced-in territory within which you live. This territory is defined by three factors: the situations, processes, and relationships that fill your life. By *situations* we mean the circumstances in which you spend your time. These can include your job, your community, your church, your clubs or organizations, and so on. By *relationships* we mean not only your most intimate partnerships, but also the other people in your life: family, friends, colleagues, and acquaintances. By *processes* we mean the ways that you treat yourself—the labels that you place on yourself, the way that you treat your body and spirit, and the way that you generally live your life.

Within this territory, couples who practice BEST fill their lives as much as possible with what stress researcher Suzanne Kobasa calls the three Cs of stress hardiness: involvements that *challenge*, to which we are *committed*, and over which we have some sense of *control*. This can mean managing career changes, dealing with aging, raising a family, facing health problems, or keeping intimacy alive in marriage.

The first step in BEST is to ask a profoundly simple question: Does the territory of our lives have a toxic or nurturing effect?

By *toxic* we mean anything that makes you feel miserable, frightened, anxious, generally uncomfortable, or stuck in a painfully familiar emotional struggle. By *nurturing* we mean anything that makes you feel reasonably safe, appreciated, acknowledged, secure, and energized.

It's impossible to thrive unless the situations, relationships, and processes that structure your days create a nurturing fence around the territory of your life. We often counsel people who are courageously willing to endure living in the thin air of stress, but who balk at changing anything about their territory. When our clients gets stuck like this, we tell them the tale of the *traffic dodger.*

We explain that their way of enduring toxic situations, processes, or relationships puts them on a par with people who regularly get smashed by some zooming vehicle because they make their livings by dodging traffic in the middle of a busy intersection. If traffic dodgers come to us seeking help with stress management or lost passion in their marriages, our first bit of advice is to encourage them to get themselves out of harm's way. We emphasize that dodging traffic all day is not a very normal way to live. Only once they find the courage to change the territory in which they live will they be able to get an accurate picture of their problems.

How Do You Compare?

If you are like most of us, your life will improve if you find the courage to change something about the situations, relationships, or processes that structure your days. Even if you can't or won't change the circumstances of your life, there is hope. Stress-hardy people manage their lives by managing themselves. They deal with stress from the inside out. Controlling their own attitudes, coping tendencies, and relationship dynamics, they disrupt coping patterns that otherwise would occur reflexively and thereby hurt themselves and their relationships. The first step is to slow things down.

Chapter Three

The "Ready, Set, Go" Relationship

In addition to new forms, today's relationships also suffer from a new pace. Hurry sickness is our most prevalent malady.

The Time of Our Lives

We seem confused about our relationships with time—a commodity that we grapple to gain, struggle to find, battle to control, and never manage to master. In days gone by we lived at a slower pace marked by biological rhythms of nature. Today, "we live by the frenetic technological rhythms of the cybernetic clock, the constant, staccato, uneven beat of computer and fax, telephone and television, stop-and-start traffic, security alarm and beepers." These gadgets are supposed to save us time; in truth, they simply speed us up, shorten our tasks, and leave us constantly invaded and rushed by demands from the world outside.

Physician Stephan Rechtschaffen, cofounder and director of the Omega Institute for Holistic Studies, noted that we race through what he calls life's *in-between* time: walking from the car to the office, carpooling our kids to dance lessons, and so on. "We start to believe that life is lived somewhere else, in another strata of time . . . In our rush to join the rich and famous, our culture forgets that the bulk of life is wonderfully mundane. That's the part that matters in the long run." But in our hurry to get to the next task, we seldom have the opportunity to bask in the mundane.

When Is It Time for Family?

Time is a major source of disorientation and anger in families. Family time is perceived as a distraction from other pursuits. Especially among the middle class and the affluent, everyone in the family has a hectic schedule and the schedules rarely mesh. "As a family, we [have become] out of synch with one another, like a small orchestra in which each musician plays a different tune to a different beat—all of them way too fast." A family shapes itself through the time it spends together. At the most basic level, if there is no family time, it can be argued that there is no family.

How often do you use your time to enhance your relationships? To do so, you must embrace what Dr. Michele Ritterman calls "the inefficient use of time—for touching one another, for just being with one another, for connecting based on how it feels to be together."

Instead, most of us juxtapose life on the run with periods of vegging out while trying to recover from our Big Life. Forty percent of leisure time is spent in front of the television or venting anger at the way we spend time the rest of the week. The average working couple in America spends only 20 minutes a day sharing time together. The major fuel of hurry sickness is work addiction.

Work Addiction

We have never counseled people rehabilitating from anything who did not question how and why they worked as they did. Indeed, work seems to have become "our magnificent obsession."

Work can serve and enslave us in many ways. It can become our main source of meaning. It can fulfill emotional needs for power, security, identity, and sense of self. It can provide excitement and a sense of possibility about the future. For some, working wards off anxiety or depression and gives them tangible proof of their worth and place in the world. Work can also provide a refuge from personal struggles and give a sense of purpose and control. For many, coworkers have replaced community, church, and extended family; the workplace is their only place of connection and most consistent source of feedback.

We are cautioned that we will likely not complete our careers with companies that currently employ us. We are advised that the way to cope with downsizing anxiety is to be self-reliant, develop ever expanding skills, learn other people's jobs, focus on making ourselves irreplaceable to our companies, and forge ahead. In short, become workaholics.

Some management gurus even explicitly propose hurrying and workaholism as keys to success. For example, consultant Mark McCormick recommends never wasting time reading the morning newspaper.

Even worse, the ever popular management guru, Tom Peters, cautioned:

> We have found that the majority of passionate activists . . . have given up family vacation, Little League games, birthday dinners, evenings, weekends, and lunch hours, gardening, reading, movies, and most other pastimes . . . We are frequently asked if it is possible

to have it all—a full and satisfying personal life and a full and satisfying hard-working professional one. Our answer is: No. The price of excellence is time, attention, and focus.

Many of us take this advice to heart. We have normalized rushing and work addiction. People from all stations of life are working longer and harder than ever. In a 1990 *Fortune* magazine survey of CEOs, 58 percent said that they expect high-level executives to work 50 to 59 hours per week, and 53 percent expect middle managers to put in those same hours. Another 62 percent reported that they have to work longer hours than they did ten years ago, with 45 percent spending between 60 and 69 hours per week at the job.

In *The Overworked American*, author Juliet Schor points out that compared to 15 years ago, the average American employee now spends an extra 163 hours on the job per year—the equivalent of an extra month of work each year.

In general, we all seem to be working more and playing less. Americans, on average, vacation only two weeks. A 1995 survey by the marketing unit for Hilton Hotels found that 38 percent of people interviewed had not taken any vacation in more than a year. Even more sobering: 27 percent of those who did vacation were nervous about their work while on vacation, and 19 percent said they couldn't stop thinking about work while on vacation. Thirteen percent actually took work along with them.

The New Work Addiction: Daily Acts of Heroism

What is not often studied is the workaholism of those driven millions who do not spend endless hours at the office, but who do work their lives away. We are referring here to the many superachieving men and women who work excessively in their combined roles.

They manage their relationships, their homes, their hobbies, their avocational involvements, and, often, their for-pay work. More than any others, working mothers are plagued by this syndrome. Estimates are that the average working mother spends anywhere from 65 to 95 hours per week in her combined roles. In *The Second Shift*, Arlie Hochschild pointed out that noncareer working women who cannot afford to hire an extensive support system to help manage their homes are among the most driven members of our culture. According to Hochschild, because of their multiple roles women today, compared to a generation ago, work an *extra month of twenty-four-hour days a year*.

One of the most painful mistakes made by supercouples is failure to notice their own or their partner's heroics. Those heroic acts include taking out the trash, driving the carpool, preparing the taxes, keeping track of birthdays, calling the repairman, and hundreds of other routine labors. People are amazingly resilient if given at least a little reinforcement for their efforts. But they become demoralized if they simply toil without appreciation. So make a concerted effort to notice daily acts of heroism: by your colleagues and their families; by your loved ones; and, most of all, when looking in the mirror.

Whether it is an official job or one of our many roles, we often end up working too hard at it. For some of us, this is due to an actual addiction to work. For others, it's a choice.

Are You a Workaholic or a Compulsive Worker?

- Constant hurrying
- Relentless need to stay busy
- Excessive need to control others

- Perfectionism
- Difficulty with relationships
- Regularly engaging in work binges: Work highs lead to work hangovers, complete with symptoms of withdrawal, anxiety, and depression
- Concealing work binges to avoid disapproval from others
- Difficulty relaxing and having fun
- Exhaustion and preoccupation with planning and work resulting in brownouts during which the details of life are overlooked: conversations, exits off the interstate, appointments
- Impatience and irritability
- Feelings of inadequacy unless working
- Self-neglect in deference to the need to keep working

According to work addictions expert Bryan Robinson, this list specifies how work addiction looks and feels. Are you work addicted? What about your partner? The Work Addiction Risk Test for Couples, on pages 27 through 29, will help you find out.

Maybe It's Compulsion; Not Addiction

In their book *He Works/She Works™: Successful Strategies for Working Couples*, career coaches and consultants Drs. Jaine and James Carter propose that true workaholism differs from compulsive working. True workaholics *prefer* work to interpersonal involvement. They work because they *love* to work.

Compulsive workers, on the other hand, work because they feel they *have* to. They are pushed by anxieties, excessive needs for perfection, or their own discomfort with relaxing. The test from *He Works/ She Works™* on page 30 will help you assess yourself in this regard.

THE WORK ADDICTION RISK
TEST FOR COUPLES[1]

Instructions:

a. Read each of the following statements below and decide how much each one pertains to you and to your partner.

> NOTE: In responding, be sure to interpret *work* as your life's work—that combination of obligations, roles, and responsibilities that you feel are part of your job.

b. Use the following rating scale:

1	2	3	4
Never true	*Sometimes true*	*Often true*	*Always true*

c. Tally your respective total scores.

Scores:

MINE	YOURS	
____	____	1. I prefer to do most things myself rather than ask for help.
____	____	2. I get impatient when I have to wait for someone else or when something takes too long, such as long slow-moving lines.
____	____	3. I seem to be in a hurry and racing against the clock.
____	____	4. I get irritated when I am interrupted while I am in the middle of something.
____	____	5. I stay busy and keep many irons in the fire.

[1] This is a modification by Wayne and Mary Sotile of the Work Addiction Risk Test in Bryan Robinson (1997), *Chained to the Desk: A Guidebook for Workaholics, Their Partners and Children and the Clinicians Who Treat Them.* New York: New York University Press.

continued

MINE	YOURS	
——	——	6. I find myself doing two or three things at one time, such as eating lunch and writing a memo, while talking on the phone.
——	——	7. I overcommit myself by biting off more than I can chew.
——	——	8. I feel guilty when I am not working on something.
——	——	9. It is important that I see the concrete results of what I do.
——	——	10. I am more interested in the final results of my work than in the process.
——	——	11. Things just never seem to move fast enough or get done fast enough for me.
——	——	12. I lose my temper when things don't go my way or work out to suit me.
——	——	13. I ask the same question, without realizing it, after I've already been given the answer.
——	——	14. I spend a lot of time mentally planning and thinking about future events, while tuning out the here and now.
——	——	15. I find myself continuing to work after my coworkers have called it quits.
——	——	16. I get angry when people don't meet my standards of perfection.
——	——	17. I get upset when I am in situations that I cannot control.
——	——	18. I tend to put myself under pressure with self-imposed deadlines.
——	——	19. It is hard for me to relax when I'm not working.
——	——	20. I spend more time working than socializing with friends, on hobbies, or on leisure activities.

continued

MINE   *YOURS*

____   ____   21. I dive into projects to get a head start before all the phases have been finalized.

____   ____   22. I get upset with myself for making even the smallest mistake.

____   ____   23. I put more thought, time, and energy into my work than I do into my relationships with my partner, friends, and loved ones.

____   ____   24. I forget, ignore, or minimize important family celebrations such as birthdays, reunions, anniversaries, or holidays.

____   ____   25. I make important decisions before I have all the facts and have a chance to think them through thoroughly.

TOTALS:
MINE   YOURS

____   ____

SCORING:

25–56 = You are not work addicted.

57–66 = You are mildly work addicted.

67–100 = You are highly work addicted.

Process points:

- Note how you each define your own and each other's work.
- Note where you agree and disagree in self- and other-ratings.
- Note changes in your perceptions of each other: Have you changed in ways that your partner doesn't recognize?
- Note small changes in your own and your partner's work style or work orientation that might make a difference in the quality of your day-to-day life together.

WORKAHOLIC OR COMPULSIVE WORKER?

Instructions: Choose the statement in each pair that best describes how you feel.

1. a. I stay after working hours to get caught up.
   b. I get so caught up in my work that I forget the time.
2. a. I get bored if I don't keep busy.
   b. I would rather be working than interacting.
3. a. I stay busy with all of my responsibilities.
   b. I enjoy the challenge of my work.
4. a. I prefer vacations with many activities.
   b. I prefer vacations that can be combined with work.
5. a. I feel guilty if I'm not working.
   b. I find it difficult to envision a life without work.
6. a. I feel anxious about work.
   b. I feel most alive when I am working.
7. a. Many times I am too busy and exhausted to have sex.
   b. It is difficult for me to concentrate on making love when I am involved in a project.
8. a. I would rather do things myself than risk someone else's mistake.
   b. I do things myself because I like to stay involved.
9. a. I will pass up social events if I have work to do.
   b. I would rather work than go to a social event.
10. a. I would rather work than argue.
    b. I am too involved in work to have time to disagree.

Interpretations: According to the Carters, if you answered *b* to six or more statements, you may be a workaholic who works because you want to. If you chose *a* for six or more statements, your work is more compulsive. You work because you feel you have to.

© Jaine M. Carter (1-800-566-6155)

The High-Powered Triad

Regardless of what we call it, the pace and load we manage is excessive. Our swirl of role changes, insecure careers, and hurry sickness lead us into Type A behavior patterns (TYABP). You are Type A if you are stuck in a lifestyle of struggling: aggressively pushing to achieve more and more in less and less time, justifying your struggle with the worldview that the environment is a hostile or limiting place filled with incompetent people. Any person who is placed in the wrong situation long enough will develop this coping style. Some people develop certain aspects of TYABP and not others; some only show TYABP in certain situations. But 70 percent of us develop at least one Type A coping habit. Super-achieving Type As are especially prone to revolve around a triad of roles: superperson, shamed, and angry.

The Superperson State

Most of us spend most of our time here. Our lives expand and we juggle multiple roles, tasks, and projects. We go numb and assume superperson levels of responsibilities and obligations. Accomplishing one goal or finishing one project simply leads to our refocusing on the next. We stay charged up with our high standards, abundant energy, and ambition. We fill our days with hard-driving effort, superefficiency, and conscientiousness. We structure our time by relentlessly focusing on and pursuing our goals. In the process, we fail to monitor signs of increasing mental or physical fatigue. We grow ever more numb and become increasingly prone to burnout and overly sensitive to any setbacks or criticism.

Living this way can blur our awareness of what is reasonable. This point has been poignantly made in studies of female university faculty members. Despite working between 86 and 107 hours per week at home and work, such women tend to *not* consider themselves overworked! As one researcher put it:

> Not only did they not acknowledge that they were overworked, they also took for granted that they ought to be able to accept their dual role without complaint. In not admitting they were overworked, these women felt they could and should be able to be feminine, successful in their careers, good mothers, and have happy marriages—all without feeling overloaded.

Shamed

We have the superperson stuff down pat; we have become proficient at going numb and keeping on going. But we falter in dealing with the second leg of the triad—the complex emotions that surface when our superperson armor is chinked. This conglomerate of emotions can be referred to as *shame.*

Here, *shame* is defined as a sense of inadequacy or exposure in which the sense of self is in danger of being flooded or overwhelmed with powerful feelings—usually anger, sorrow, or love. Shame crops up when we feel we are failing at superperson tasks or when our yearnings for connection and contact seem counter to what we should feel and how we should behave. "Shame means the *failure to live up to* one's inner ideals."

Struggles to balance independence and affiliation inevitably lead to some degree of shame. Men feel shame when their mask of independence is pushed away, and they experience vulnerability and other feminine states such as fear, anxiety, or sadness. These dark emotions predictably surface in the wake of the swirl of changes in the contemporary work world. They are, however, not comfortable emotions for most men.

As we will discuss later, the effects of a high-powered lifestyle on women are equally severe. Women feel shame when their connection with significant others is limited, either by their assertion of their own needs or, more typically, by the demands placed on them by the Big Life.

And the negative effects of women's expanded roles are not just emotional in nature. The strains that fill women's lives tend to damage their relationships and their health. For example, female physicians are 40 percent more prone to divorce than their male colleagues. Women doctors also live, on average, ten years less than their female counterparts in nonprofessional occupations.

In different ways, the Big Life creates shame for today's men and women. As *both* genders harbor a sense of inadequacy, the stage is set for bouncing back and forth between superperson and angry roles.

Angry

Faced with the pain of shame, high-powered people tend to do one of two things: They distract themselves by switching back to the superperson state or move into the angry state.

Being angry hurts less than being scared, or shamed, or sad. For many, the dynamic in their primary relationships makes it an easy target for their anger. The lost intimacy, dwindling nurturance, and rampant stress that characterizes their relationships make it easy to blame their coconspirator in creating the Big Life.

Often, anger is fueled when we are abandoned by our most private audience, the person on whom we depend for emotional sustenance. Criticizing your partner's ability to relate, parent, love, or provide not only shatters the superperson state, it dismantles the other person's very sense of self.

In our counseling sessions with high-powered people, we have noticed that this kind of hurting comes in many forms:

The only reason we don't enjoy life more is that you are not ambitious enough. Look at our friends, they manage to stay busy and enjoy the good things in life.

Wife of a man who earns $125,000 per year.

I'll tell you what my misery is about. I'm miserably alone. If you were more involved in this family, maybe our marriage would have a chance.

Wife of a man who works 70 hours per week in his profession and 35 hours per week attending to his children and his home responsibilities.

Our daughter is wetting the bed because her mother is off closing deals rather than tucking her in, reading to her, and saying a prayer with her at night.

Husband of a woman realtor whose income is necessary for their livelihood.

What did you expect me to do? We have sex once a month if I force the issue. All you do is mope around, exhausted all the time. Of course I looked elsewhere.

Husband of a mother of three young children, following his being caught in an extramarital affair.

Mismanaged anger is a prevalent problem in today's world. We will extensively discuss strategies for managing anger in Chapter Eleven.

Chronic hurrying and work addiction are integrally related, and these twin dynamics take their toll on our health, productivity, and quality of life. Like any addict, a work addict gives up control. People who believe they have no control over the pace and conditions of their life suffer drops in self-confidence and have higher levels of stress.

Mismanaged hurry sickness and work addiction are the major, untreated causes of much that ails contemporary families. When we burn out, we damage not only our careers, but also our loved ones.

Chapter Four

When Hunters Nest and Nesters Hunt

We are a new breed of couples. We are overwhelmingly stressed; but we are clear about the causes of our stress. Our dilemma lies in the effects of the Big Life that violate the divergent needs shared by both sexes—the need for feeling attached enough and the need for feeling independent enough.

Today's men and women have joined ranks formerly occupied exclusively by the other gender. Women are now driven as only men used to be, and are suffering the consequences of being aggressive architects of expanded lives. Men are puzzled as to the reason security at work and connection at home keep eluding them. They are also frustrated with the perceived lack of nurturing they receive from the women in their lives. Women are puzzled as to the reason success at work seems to come at the cost of connection at home. They are also frustrated, unable to find a comfortable-enough place and pace in the Big Life that has become their new normal.

The Original Drama

It used to be simple. A woman's job was to find a man who could use a stick well enough to hunt for food and provide protection. In turn, she would take care of the shelter, gather food, and raise the children.

Despite our heightened sensibilities and raised consciousness, the caveman and cavewoman drives still pull at us. According to a 1996 cover series by *GQ*, the primary drivers for women are security, love, commitment, and connection; men want sex.

Feminist researchers Carol Gilligan and Nancy Chodorow proposed that intimacy issues stem, for most of us, from having as our first powerful caretaker a female—mother. The fact that this first object of attachment is of the same sex for a little girl and of the opposite sex for a little boy leads to gender differences in the ways identity is formed. It also affects how comfortable we are in relationships.

Being the same sex as mother leads a girl to define herself in terms of attachment to significant others. Then she is socialized to develop abilities that make her comfortable in relationships: she learns to be aware of emotions, to talk about feelings, and to show affection. These influences run so deeply in a woman that her identity and sense of self may be threatened if she is left to function too independently *unless this push for individuality or autonomy is made with the support of harmonious relationships.* Boys, on the other hand, are socialized to create identity around independence and expressions of individuality. Only when their identities are firmly established can most men function comfortably in intimate relationships.

These developmental dramas are further complicated by the marital dynamics into which we are born. Author and poet Robert Bly points out that many contemporary men were reared in father-absent families. Due to their father's military service, workaholism, other addictions, or simple emotional unavailability, many boys are reared in family situations that charge them with the task of fulfilling the needs and expectations of a mother who is frustrated with the emotional and physical absence of her husband. Such a demand can stir taboos that may lead a boy to seek the safety of emotional isolation and to further focus on learning to operate in the world outside of the family. His inner needs for intimacy and solace are saved for that one true love whom he will one day find *if he can just become successful enough.*

As a result, when it comes to balancing autonomy and affiliation, men and women enter relationships with quite different needs. The woman searches for attachment enough and the man searches for independence enough to feel fulfilled and capable of coping.

The Midlife Crossover

It used to be that only late in life did women express their individuality and men push for intimacy. Only when the kids were raised, the husband ensconced in his own career, and her nest tidily in order, was she ready to express her independent self. At the same time, with his identity clearly in place ("I've got the right job, right number of kids, right wife, right lawn mower, all the right stuff."), at midlife *he* was ready for intimacy; but she was going off to school, starting her own business, or otherwise declaring her individuality.

A New Twist: Let's Both Do It!

The sexual revolution and dramatic reshuffling in the workplace have changed the old-time bargaining dance. Now, both genders go for independence and sexual involvement early in the relationship, and both need the other's help to feel successful enough and loved enough. For a relationship to work today, each partner must do two things crucial to the other's self-esteem: validate the partner's competence and fulfill the other's needs for connection, security, nurturing, and intimacy.

The surprising news is how distressing this new deal is for *both* sexes. We all struggle for more individuality, and we all want more compassion and nurturing—a role typically female—but neither gender seems to be comfortable with the balance between independence and connection. Both sexes lament the loss of the nurturing element early in busy marriages; couples become good at a corporate or managerial style, but have little time left to emotionally validate each other. The consequences of this erosion in support can be devastating for both sexes.

What Burns Out Women?

Research clearly shows that caring connection with loved ones is necessary for women to remain stress resistant. The flip side of this is also true: the fastest way to promote burnout in women is to put them in relationships that lack intimacy and are filled with conflict. When that is the case, women grow depressed, socially withdraw, and suffer various aches and pains.

By choice or default, today's women are bombarded by a second factor that damages their well-being: excessive work responsibilities. Women's burgeoning presence in a world formerly occupied by male hunters yields bittersweet outcomes. To a point, an increased degree of job involvement correlates with increased self-esteem for both men and women. Beyond that point, increased job involvement results in further increases in self-worth for men, but in *diminished* self-esteem for women.

It has been documented that high-powered women report more emotional distress and frustration, poorer physical health, poorer marital adjustments, less self-esteem, and more general unhappiness than do more passive women. Those women who identify with a more traditionally feminine role and lifestyle seem to especially suffer negative effects of a high-powered lifestyle. On the other hand, women who are characterized as highly career involved and who show high levels of masculinity (as measured by a standardized sex role inventory) report higher levels of self-esteem and less depression than their counterparts who are both career involved and more feminine.

It may be that societal prohibitions against females showing their own high-powered capabilities are the culprits that hurt those women who are more feminine in their orientation. It also may be that more feminine women are simply more honest and accurate than either their male counterparts or their more macho female counterparts in identifying the stresses that come with the Big Life.

Do Men Really Want More Connection?

Do men really want more nurturing, or are they still simply in pursuit of more sex, more stuff, and more job security? Recent research by Wellesley College psychologist Rosalind Barnett, Ph.D., and her colleagues strongly argues that no differences exist in the importance of family life to married men and women. These researchers studied 300 dual-career couples and found that job stresses have equal effects on men's and women's mental health and, most interestingly, that men are "almost as strongly committed to the family role as are women."

Our own experiences in counseling thousands of couples have also led us to conclude that today's men are not only interested in, but also capable of participating in nurturing relationships. How can this be, given that we are supposedly a generation of males who were reared in father-absent families? As one of our male clients explained it: "Where did I learn about being a nurturing man? I'll tell you: I learned it from Beaver Cleaver's family and from Andy Griffith. As a kid, I watched television all the time. Now, believe me, I know now and I knew then that the pictures of family life those TV shows painted weren't real; my family sure wasn't that way. But watching shows like *Beaver* and *Andy Griffith* taught me something about how nurturing men acted. It made a difference in my life."

Whether from television, education, or lessons taught by the women in their lives, most men today have learned to be more aware of their own and their loved ones' needs. But what good does it do them when their busy lives so often drain them and thwart their own and their partners' abilities to participate in their relationships?

A Second Twist: Who's Got the Power?

Changes in our work world have led to a revolution in our bedrooms. Margaret Mead said,

> In every known human society, everywhere in the world, the young male learns that when he grows up, one of the things which he must do in order to be a full member of society is to provide food for some female and her young.

If her words are true, then we have a serious problem. Most men today are not able to hunt well enough by themselves to provide for and protect their families, and this truth is disrupting the age-old dance between the sexes.

Between 1987 and 1994, 85 percent of *Fortune* 1,000 companies downsized, to the tune of over two-million lay-offs each year. In 1994, the *New York Times* reported that three of four people surveyed had either lost a job or benefits or were close to someone who had. The downsizing craze has led to a generation of work-anxious, work-battered couples.

An invisible result of corporate downsizing is the mushrooming number of relationships left suffering from the plight of an over-functioning woman and an underfunctioning man. Regardless of how high powered they may be, both men and women tend to struggle when *his* career and *their* marriage take backseats to the status, prestige, income, and time demands of *her* life. We will elaborate on the inner workings of such couples in Chapter Five. Here, we set the backdrop for that discussion.

The wife earns more than her husband in 18 percent of American households. Recent studies show that between 30 and 40 percent of college-educated working women earn more than their spouses.

Despite huge social changes during the past 30 years, traditional attitudes prevail. *The Economist* found that more than two-thirds of Europeans (ranging from 85 percent in Germany to 60 percent in Denmark) thought it better for the mother of a young child to stay at home than a father. Yet the number of at-home fathers is rising. In America it rose from 61,000 in 1975 to 257,000 in 1990. While this form of role reversal is welcomed by some, it goes against the grain for many people. After all, since the days of the cavemen, the man has been the one expected to wield the big stick.

We encourage you to explore your own attitudes in this area. Do you harbor prejudices regarding stay-at-home mothers versus stay-at-home fathers? Imagine a neighborhood where most of the women do not work outside their homes for pay. Jot down the images that this brings to mind.

Now, think of a neighborhood where most men are jobless, and note your mental images again.

If you are like most people, the first fantasy conjures visions of tidy homes and children at play in picket-fenced yards. The notion of jobless men at home, on the other hand, tends to stir more sinister pictures.

Indeed, our culture strongly associates responsibility and marriage with men who are employed. Unmarried men commit more crime; employed men are far more likely to marry and parent responsibly. It is still true that if a man is not a good hunter, he doesn't remain in society's good graces.

New Variants of Marriage and Family Life

We are a generation of pioneers charting new cultural paths. Sometimes, the new territory we chart is literal as well as figurative. Relocation due to career moves creates stress for many Dynamic Duos and their families.

For most couples, this issue raises a complicated set of questions: What will happen to your spouse's career? Whose turn is it to have his or her career deferred to? How does this decision relate to the rule in your relationship regarding whose career will be most important? Is the change you are considering worth the hassles it will cause to all parties concerned? Are you willing to pay the price of not accepting the transfer?

Commuter Marriage

A solution to the transfer issue is one partner living apart from the family during stints of work. This is most often intended to be a temporary arrangement, implemented as a way of determining whether the new job will work out before uprooting the family. However, some families settle into this arrangement as a permanent lifestyle. The result is two separate lives: the one they have together and the one they have apart.

We recently worked with a couple who grew so accustomed to their commuter marriage that they chose to continue it, even after the original reasons for living apart (the kids) grew up and left home. For over 35 years and through three major career moves by the husband, they have maintained their weekend marriage and family life. And both partners swear that they have been faithful to each other.

The major hurdles faced by commuter marriages are communication, cohesion, and expectations. Because commuter couples don't see each other much, communication tends to be disjointed and connections between the commuter and the other family members weaken. In addition, commuter couples tend to have honeymoon-like expectations of each other, expectations that are often not lived up to.

Frequent-Flyer Marriages

Paul and Sue have been married for 13 years. Each has a senior-level position with a major pharmaceutical company. They spend on average 218 nights each year in hotels. Their problem? They are very seldom both in the *same* hotel or even in the same state.

Extensive work travel brings its own stresses and challenges to families. Travelers learn firsthand that the only people who believe that traveling is glamorous are people who don't do it much. Those who travel extensively complain of loneliness, fatigue, and a feeling of being uprooted.

Yet extensive travelers also grow accustomed to the fast pace, high stimulation, and solitary time that comes with traveling. They acclimate to making brief, intense contact with others, followed by lengthy periods of disconnection as they rush off to their next meeting or assignment. When they get together as a couple, their day-to-day routines get disassembled, and they have to readjust to sharing time and space with another.

Working Separate Shifts

From 1980 to 1988 the percentage of dual-career couples jumped from 52 to 63 percent, and the figure has risen steadily over the past decade. It is now estimated that in over 70 percent of couples, both spouses work. To manage their juggling act, many couples work separate shifts. This is a solution for some two-income couples and an unwanted necessity for others. Alice and Tom are examples of the first case: "We hate not seeing each other much during the week. But working separate shifts is the only way that we can raise our children ourselves. We don't live near family, and we refuse to leave our kids at daycare while they are this young."

Other couples face the reality that separate shift jobs are a necessity. "After 13 years of shift work, I finally got promoted to supervisor," explained Milo. "Problem is, it's a third-shift position. But, hey, we need the money. I'm not complaining."

These families deal with the effects of different biological rhythms, sleep patterns, and a weekend marriage pattern. Their challenge is to frequently enough create islands of time when both have energy to stay awake and participate in family life.

Working Together

One out of every six middle managers and executives who lose their jobs as the result of downsizing start their own small companies, many with their spouses. As codirectors of our own practice and speaking business, we are well acquainted with the joys and stresses that come with this marital twist.

Three major stresses face couples who work together: setting limits on the extent that work dominates the relationship; establishing clear role divisions at work; and bearing through the expanded glimpses each partner gets of the other relative to most couples.

The first two problems are obvious: If the co-owner of your business climbs into bed with you each night, it is far more likely that work will invade your personal space than if your co-owner beds with someone else. "We became partners in our business and lost our romance" is a sentiment expressed by many of our marriage counseling clients who work together. Second, couples who work together successfully have to decide who will be the boss in which areas of the business and respect each other's authority in those areas.

The third challenge is more complex. When working together allows glimpses of each other's Achilles heel, it is easy to lose patience and respect for each other. One of our clients expressed it well:

> It was one thing to hear my husband complain about the problems at the office when he was working for a big architectural firm. It's another thing to see him bumble his way through mismanaging our secretary and then have to listen to him complain about her work. Now I see how he creates the circumstances that he feels victimized by, and it's hard for me to not criticize him and be disappointed in him. If we didn't work together, this would be one problem we would not have.

Working at Home

Forty-million Americans currently work from home, and this number will rise to sixty million by the end of 1998. Telecommuting is also becoming a booming option. Even the government now is allowing certain workers to perform their jobs from their homes. According to the U.S. Chamber of Commerce, more than 25 million workers list their home address as their office address. Estimates are that by the year 2000, one-third of the American workforce will be telecommuting from home.

The stresses that come with working at home result from the failure to set work time boundaries, and the dilemmas presented by the conflicting demands of work and family.

At-home workers certainly do enjoy the advantages of a flexible work schedule and less pressure and expense to dress for work. But this option also requires a great deal of family cooperation and participation. The home becomes a place that is invaded by work, and more often than in other arrangements, family members are called on to participate in the home-worker's tasks.

Both psychological and societal factors influence how today's Dynamic Duos relate to one another. But most of the new variants of marriage and family life are determined by the effect that work has on the ways we spend our time. Obviously, couples with commuter marriages or unemployed husbands have extra hurdles to jump. But even couples who aren't facing those obstacles (right now anyway) have to deal with how work and their relationship to it effects their union.

Chapter Five

Superachievers and the Men and Women Who Love Them

Do We Want to Connect or Disconnect?

Men and women have learned to better understand each other over the past 30 years, but we continue to struggle with each other. As our Big Life tensions mount, haunting self-doubts begin to surface.

> Maybe my husband is right: I'm just not playful enough. It seems harder than ever to just relax and enjoy being home. More and more, I seem to need that little help to switch gears—a few drinks or glasses of wine.
>
> *Ann, a computer consultant*

> Maybe my wife is right: I'm not open enough. I feel compassion and concern for her, but I keep hearing that I just don't communicate well. It's as though we are speaking different languages.
>
> *Glenn, an attorney*

> Maybe I'm not nurturing enough. We all know that I love my kids. I rearrange my life to attend most of their games and school events.

But they seem to be so much more connected with their mother than they are with me.

David, a construction worker

Maybe I am too ambitious. Other people seem to be more content with less; I seem to be driven. And my family is telling me that they miss me.

Lois, a marketing executive

Both men and women are vulnerable to anxieties that make them ambivalent about connecting. They want and need support from each other but feel ashamed of their struggles, and this shame makes them question if they deserve connection or know how to connect. A strange form of teamwork then develops. It's called the *pursuer-distancer dance*.

The Pursuer-Distancer Dance

We have never met a couple who did not engage in some version of this dance: Partner A is constantly asking for more affection, conversation, connection, and time with the other. Partner B seems stuck in the habit of distancing with fatigue, numbness, pre-occupation, or activity. The more the pursuer pursues, the more the distancer distances. Eventually, the pursuer gets fed up and gives up.

Next, the partners momentarily switch roles: the pursuer starts to distance and the distancer starts to pursue. This dance lasts until connection is made, and then the roles revert back to form: Partner B returns to distancing and partner A again pursues. It's as though the couple were stuck in a dance similar to that of two magnets of like poles that scoot away as the other approaches.

What Causes This Dance?

The fuel for the pursuer-distancer dance is anxiety. On the one hand, there is anxiety about losing connection with each other. On the other hand, there is anxiety about facing aspects of themselves that only get stirred by long-term, intimate relationships. Some distancers avoid this self-confrontation by literally fleeing: into work, numbness, their own compulsions, or a new relationship.

We stereotypically think of men as always being the distancers in this dance. Popular writers have suggested that men tend to respond to relationship tension with a fix-it stance that conveys the message: "Let's not talk about it; let's take action." If that doesn't work, men distance. Women, on the other hand, supposedly want to discuss things and grapple with any unfinished business in the relationship.

This does seem to be the predominant, general pattern. However, we are counseling growing numbers of high-powered couples in which the woman is the distancer. The Big Life appears to be moving couples out of their typical, gender-based responses. It is no longer easy to generalize about how men and women respond to each other.

Attempted Solutions That Complicate Our Problems

Any high-powered man or woman stuck in a pursuer-distancer dance will struggle to take control of the relationship. The dialogues between conflicting partners in our offices suggest that during this struggle, they try out strategies that backfire: they defend themselves and try to influence their partners with attempted solutions that only serve to further complicate things.

We find that *both* men and women reach for some of the attempted solutions shown on pages 50 and 51—all of which drain

ATTEMPTED SOLUTION	EFFECT
Intellectualizing	Drains emotion from relationship
Shifting blame onto other person	Diverts attention from one's own discomfort
Silence	Allows illusion of control
Finding solace in isolation or withdrawal	Momentarily relieves relationship tensions
Identifying with aggressor (overly complying or agreeing with criticisms voiced by partner)	Takes wind out of partner's complaints; really puts the other in a one-down position
Projecting part of your own conflict onto another	Allows illusion that the problem really belongs to your partner, not to you
Identifying with that which your partner projects onto you	Relieves anxiety that comes from confronting uncomfortable aspects of your partner
Dominating and intimidating	Promotes illusion of power, autonomy, and importance, but blocks authentic connection
Physical violence or verbal abuse	Masks a burning inadequacy about intimacy and a deep sense of insignificance and helplessness in dealing with loved ones
Passive aggression	Allows supposedly one-down partner to control relationship through passive resistance

continued

Infidelity	Damages trust if infidelity is discovered. If infidelity is not discovered, drains relationship of energy caused by undisclosed secret
Overfocusing on logic	Causes loss of emotional empathy and ability to nurture others
Playing on sympathy of loved ones by refusing to take responsibility for curbing addictive behaviors	Paralyzes loved ones in codependent roles and prevents resolution of issues

intimacy from the relationship. Which of the roles describes you? Which describes your partner?

If you or your partner is stuck in any of these attempted solutions or postures, recognize them as stress reactions, not indictments of your character. Something about the way you are living, dealing with each other, or mismanaging yourself is stirring you to defend yourself in these ways.

The struggles of supercouples are exposed by the laments of their partners. We will discuss these from the perspectives of both men and women.

The Pursuer-Distancer Dance: The Man's Perspective

Men distance in relationships for two reasons, both having to do with mismanaged shame. In the first scenario, the relationship feels like a place filled with high demands over which he has low control. This is the most toxic form of stress, and it describes how many high-powered men experience life, both in their work and in their private lives. When unable to control what is happening, many men withdraw into silence. Others distract themselves or divert attention from themselves by focusing on irrelevant details of an argument, seeming to ignore the spirit of the message being sent.

Paul's reactions during confrontations by his wife, Patricia, are an example of this form of distancing.

> *Patricia:* What drives me crazy is that Paul won't even give me the respect of paying attention to what I'm saying when we are discussing things that he doesn't want to hear. Sometimes I feel as though I need to lock us in a room with no TV remote control to fiddle with, no windows to stare out of, no magazines to thumb through—just him and me. But even then, it wouldn't work: He would just latch on to some detail in what I'd say, and—using his lawyer's skills—he would argue it to death. I never get the satisfaction of feeling that I get my *real* points across during these discussions. It drives me crazy.

> *Paul:* What am I supposed to do during these discussions? When Patricia starts in on me like that, I feel like a trapped animal that someone is pounding on. I swear, if I didn't do something to distract myself, I think I would explode!

The second scenario that leads a man to distance himself is quite different. Here, the closeness of an intimate relationship leaves him feeling dependent, incompetent, and awkward. Many men are confused over their conflicting needs: They fear attachment, but they also fear loneliness. Remember that for men, identity is first formed through separation not attachment. Men can thus be shamed by the depth of solace they experience in an intimate relationship. The result? They create distance to momentarily alleviate the bitter-sweet discomfort that comes with connection.

As was explained by Sam Osherson in his wonderful book *Wrestling with Love: How Men Struggle with Intimacy, with Women, Children, Parents, and Each Other,* "Many men are so humiliated at their wish to be mothered that they get angry and provoke fights when they feel most in need of help and support."

This shame is often what is going on beneath the surface when a man abruptly withdraws from intimate connection. Again, Dr. Osherson:

> Shame around love—shame aroused by the yearning to be valued by and valuing of others—often makes men unwilling to see or to speak or to hear in intimate situations; we want to avert our awareness from what seems humiliating ... We become quiet and preoccupied, silent or withdrawn, just at the moments that we yearn most deeply for a response.

Dilemmas for Women Who Love Superachieving Men

When a man distances, the stage is set for his female partner to attempt to close the gap. These attempts can take several forms and result in a number of complications.

Go Play Golf. Please!

When a superachieving man drifts further and further away, his partner is likely to assume that the problem is stress. The Big Life conveniently lends itself to this interpretation, and the caretaking female offers solutions intended to soothe. "As hard as you work, you need a hobby. Why don't you make time to exercise or play golf with the guys. Please! Do something to relax."

Her hope is that if he makes time in his busy schedule to enjoy life more, his preoccupying worries and stresses will go away. He will relax and be ready to rejoin their relationship.

The risk here is that this new outlet will simply give the already distancing man yet another way to avoid the anxieties that have filled his relationship. With his typical high-powered fervor, he becomes a compulsive golfer, exerciser, sports advocate, or internet surfer. His partner then feels even more hurt and abandoned. He seems to choose to spend his passionate energies outside their relationship, and she only gets the leftovers.

Is This Codependence or Nurturing?

Several years ago, an alarm sounded throughout the pop psychology world: Beware of codependence! We were all warned, "If you don't watch out, your efforts to soothe somebody else will use up your life and just drive you crazy." The classic codependent joke:

Q: What happens at the moment of death for codependents?
A: Someone *else's* life flashes before their eyes.

Being married to a man lost in his own numbness, stress, or distancing inevitably leads to this question: Am I hurting myself by trying to help this man cope in the ways that I do?

Six months after convincing her hard-driving husband, T.J., to take better care of himself, Lindy lamented: "Now, not only does he work 65 hours each week, he plays golf 7 hours, exercises 6 hours, has to have time on Sunday mornings to read the *New York Times*—you know, to unwind from his week and keep abreast of things. He's surviving his Big Life, but killing me in the process!"

When Lindy objected to T.J.'s self-absorption, he complained of feeling trapped. "What do you want me to do? First you tell me I've got to relax more. Now you're telling me that I relax too much. What a joke! You try living my life for a while! I spend 12 hours a day pulled in 50 different directions by my company, then I come home and you pull on me to work some more. I don't think you have any idea what I go through."

This kind of confrontation stirs feelings of shame for both partners. In most relationships, what happens next is predictable: more distancing. Soon, the couple loses sight of each other.

He's Forgotten Who I Am!

Most high-powered women can tell you specifically what aspects of themselves they gave up to assume the role of nurturer and keeper of home and hearth. They may have put their careers on hold, refused promotions, interrupted their educations, or otherwise limited pursuing goals or roles that would have required spending time and energy outside the home.

During the initial years of marriage, this choice works well for most couples. Often, it's as much *her* choice to express her nurturing part as it is *his* choice that she do so. In fact, this may be part of the appeal of the relationship for a high-powered woman whose life has otherwise been focused on achieving. De-emphasizing her hunter role matches well with her gut-level stirring to create a nest and populate it with offspring.

This arrangement also tends to be satisfying to men during the relationship's early years. Even if she continues to work, the fact that his is the primary wage tends to satisfy his primitive driver to be the hunter who provides protection and food for his newly developing family.

But what starts out as a mutually satisfying contract between spouses can end up as a source of resentment. Years pass, and the couple grows accustomed to the roles they assigned and assumed.

The pursuer-distancer dance complicates the parallel process that originally works so well. Struggles such as those outlined above begin to accumulate. Eventually, their parallel course drifts into a Y, and the couple begins to lose sight of each other. One sign of this change is her lament: "You've forgotten who I am."

This was the pain-filled mantra of Chloe, who came to us for help with depression. Much of this woman's pain stemmed from the disrespectful way her husband treated her. He chided her for not being a very systematic thinker. He criticized her organizational skills. He openly complained to friends that she was irresponsible in managing money.

Her husband's constant criticism fueled Chloe's negative self-image. "It's so hard for me to feel good about myself when I'm around my husband," she complained. When asked if she recalled a time in her life when she felt more self-respect, Chloe's face brightened. "It's amazing. I never think much about who I was before I met my husband. Truth is, I was quite a hotshot in my own right. I was working for a Big Six accounting firm, solidly on a partnership tract. But I dropped out of my career to do my feminine thing. That was so long ago. Now I'm lost. I've lost a big part of myself. My husband has forgotten who I am; and so have I."

Whatever Happened to My Nurturing Husband?

Through all stages of marriage and family life, high-powered women point to support and active participation from their husbands as the single most important factor in managing the stress of their multiple roles. In a 1990 Virginia Slims opinion poll conducted by the Roper Organization, six out of ten women stated that more help from their husbands was the single biggest factor that would help them balance work and family responsibilities.

High-powered women tend to choose mates who seem willing to provide this sort of partnership. Attracted to their man's nurturing, nonsexist style, these women bask in the admiration of their female friends. They seem to have found the perfect mate; one who is nurturing and not threatened by their independence.

Their lament comes later, when they find that their nurturing husbands seem to have changed their colors. This change is reflected in a number of facts about contemporary couples:

- Between 1968 and 1988, women doubled their hours at work but decreased their hours spent in child care and housework by only 14 percent. Over this same period, men decreased their total hours at work and home by 8 percent.
- In dual-career families, employed wives continue to carry upwards of 80 percent of household and child care responsibilities, including the overall coordination of family life.
- A recent survey of nearly 3,000 randomly selected men and women found that, even in this postfeminist United States, women are still two times more likely to pay household bills than men, five times more likely to cook for the family, five times more likely to do the family shopping, and eleven times more likely to do the household cleaning. Most remarkable, these findings were true even for young couples in which the women contributed half or more of the family income.
- Even in dual-paycheck couples working separate shifts, only 18 percent of the fathers assume primary child care responsibilities during the wife's working hours.

Few men settle comfortably into the role of spouse of a super-achieving woman, if doing so means that they must assume the role of nurturer over the long term. Couples particularly struggle if the woman's individualistic pursuits prohibit her from being at least reasonably nurturing. Of course, here couples often disagree on just what *reasonably* means. Nancy and Cary were a case in point.

> When Cary and I got together, he seemed too good to be true. Not only was he not threatened by my career success; he bragged about me. He and I have truly had a partnership. He does every bit as much as I do to run our home and family. Over the years, when I have fretted that I was afraid that he might like it better if I were more domestic, he always laughed it off, saying that we had a hired housekeeper. Plus, he reminds me that it has been his choice to be a hands-on parent, not an absent father as his own dad was.
>
> But things have changed. He doesn't admit it, but he acts it. I know that he's tired of sharing the load at home the way he does. I can't exactly blame him. He's discovered what most women have always known: carpooling, parenting, and housework are not very glamorous.
>
> I don't know what to do. I am not going to quit my job. I love it, and we need the money. And I don't blame him for being fed up with his part of running our home life. He knows that I feel the same way much of the time. I accept that.
>
> But I'll tell you what I do not accept. He isn't even nice to me anymore. If he wants to change the way we parent our kids and run our house, let him say so. But his snide comments about the kind of woman and mother I am had better disappear. It's one thing for us to renegotiate how we are living. It's another for him to turn into an angry, resentful man who treats me with disrespect. I won't stand for that. I won't love him if he keeps on like this.

Overfunctioning Women/Underfunctioning Men

By choice or default, many contemporary women assume the power position in their relationships. They function as the family's mental health expert and as the relationship manager in charge of organizing the flow charts that track the family's comings and goings. Often they have their own thriving careers.

In contrast, many men remain on the periphery of the action at home and flounder in their efforts to gain a firmer stand in their work. What happens when a relationship is driven by the energy and demands of a high-powered woman?

Family researchers have long known that marriages characterized by an overfunctioning woman and underfunctioning man tend to be miserable. Both partners end up devaluing and resenting the other. Subtly or openly, *she* shames *him* for not contributing enough money, time, skill, or value. In turn, *he* shames *her* for not being feminine or nurturing enough.

Family therapist Gus Napier shed light on the inner workings of the wife-dominated marriage. Even women who are generally strong, organized, and competent yearn to be supported and emotionally fed. Some repress these needs by filling their lives with activities that focus on achievement or on satisfying the needs of others. Napier notes that, even as children, many such women essentially functioned as parents to their own parents and/or to their younger siblings.

The complimentary marital role to an overfunctioning woman, according to Napier, is the underfunctioning man who both encourages and resents his wife's competence. These men enter marriage in search of a strong, caretaking spouse who will soothe the emotional wounds caused by their own rejecting, absent, or ineffectual parents.

This pattern of overfunctioning wife/underfunctioning husband leads to various struggles. One struggle is whether he will speed up and fit into the high-powered wife's way of living. His initial admiration of her drive dovetails with her underlying hope that she will teach him to reach his potential. Whether he is underfunctioning or has reached his potential is often a matter of opinion that has serious relationship consequences. Sherry's comments show how complex this can get.

> John doesn't understand how I could have the gall to accuse him of not being ambitious. He earns $90,000 a year. He works hard. We live a nice, secure life.
>
> But I'm a real visionary; an entrepreneur at heart. He is not. I know that he's not just a *schlepp*, but I also know that he is not willing to go that extra mile that it takes to become really successful.
>
> It's not so much that I want more money; it's just that I've always been taught to do the best that I can. It seems to me that John settles for good enough when just a little bit of pushing would put him over the top.
>
> But we can't talk about this. He gets his feelings hurt, and I get angry, and we get nowhere. I don't know which of us is right.

Why Won't He Just Get a New Job?

The most painful variant of the overfunctioning woman/underfunctioning man relationship occurs when the man loses his career prestige. Worse yet is when he loses his job and fails to get another one. The syndrome: They assume that he will land on his feet; get a new, better job, or at least be able to make a parallel career move. They cling to the hope that the current situation will only be temporary.

As time marches on and he doesn't retread his career, she is left to flounder, absorbing the stress of his unemployment and trying to protect his ego by being supportive. Often, this translates into her cooperating in a refusal to discuss their stress and strain. She simply pools their money, and he manages it. Inevitably, she begins to resent the fact that he refuses to get another job—any other job.

We have never counseled a couple who were comfortable if they drastically switched the hunter/gatherer roles. No matter how much their consciousness has been raised, if they are not both working hard enough in managing their responsibilities and if he is not contributing a fair share of money to the pot, they both resent it. Jenny and Eric were caught in this dilemma.

> I know that Eric's pride is hurt. He was a victim of downsizing, which wasn't his fault. But that was nearly two years ago. We keep waiting for a new opportunity to come along. In the meantime, he has drained our savings trying one half-thought-out scheme after another. He never follows through. The money is gone. And now he wants me to ask my parents to lend us $35,000 for another business opportunity. I won't do it.
>
> I'm so ashamed about all of this. I believe in Eric; I know that his career is important to him. I know that this is a partnership, and I don't resent doing my share. But I'm losing respect for him. He gets up every day, puts on a coat and tie, and basically hangs out. He calls it networking; my father would call it loafing. My dad would have been flipping hamburgers by now; he would have gotten *some* kind of a job to help support his family.

In *He Works/She Works*, Jaine and James Carter question whether this is just another form of wife abuse. "Men who are allowing their partners to work while they make half-hearted or no attempts to contribute to the partnership are controlling women in a different way than they did in the past. In the past, men were the keepers of the money. They wrote the checks, made the investments, and delivered the allowances. Even when women earn more money, most men still control the money."

One-Downing Him at Her Own Expense

Approximately 40 percent of professional women change their career course because of family responsibilities. Women are the trailing spouse in 94 percent of job transfers in America, even when the transfer means a lessened standard of living or quality of life for the family.

We do not mean to pan these phenomena. These can be healthy choices that reflect a woman's values. Our concern is our observation that women sometimes sabotage their own careers or health in an effort to regenerate esteem for their floundering men. When a man loses status and prestige within his relationship, strange things may happen. The following examples are all drawn from our clinical practice.

At the point of being offered a partnership in her law firm, Sally began having panic attacks that led her to decide that she really wanted to work part-time.

Sally's decision to turn down her promotion happened in the wake of her husband's being rejected for partnership in his law firm. Three years later, after her husband was solidly building his own practice, Sally decided to return to full-time practice. She never had another panic attack.

Lou Ann didn't really want to resign from her career as an advertising vice president, but her chronic back pain worsened to the point that she simply could not tolerate traveling as much as her job required.

Lou Ann's back pain flared during the same year that her husband's company presented him with the ultimatum to either accept a transfer to another state or lose his position. Once they relocated, Lou Ann stayed unemployed for a year and then returned to work. She did not travel in her new position, and her back pain has remained manageable.

Karen was a housewife who suffered from Chrone's disease, a painful condition that affects the digestive system. During the 18 months prior to our meeting her, she had undergone three hospitalizations, forty-five days of bed rest, and one exploratory surgery. "The fact that my husband was out of work during this time proved to be a blessing in disguise. I don't know what we would have done if he hadn't been there to take care of me."

During the two years after her husband returned to work, Karen spent only one day in the hospital.

We fully realize that the struggles shown by these women may have resulted from many stresses other than their husbands' career dramas. But we continue to marvel at how frequently a woman's symptoms seem to reverse once her husband's career and self-esteem stabilize. It well may be that, out of a primitive desire to love and protect, women are prone to sabotage their own thriving as a way of bolstering their men's self-worth.

I Want a Real Man!

A woman's reactions to her mate's loss of power and prestige are not always so nurturing. Some, like June, look for a new partner, one who will be a more powerful collaborator in both creating and managing the Big Life.

> I know that this might not be the right thing to do, but I'm going to do it. I just don't like my life with Chuck. He is a good man, but he bores me to death. Living our little life in our little house with our little routines is just not what I want. He seems small to me. I've always liked men who sort of overwhelmed me.
>
> Jarrod excites me and I believe that I can have the kind of life with him that I've always wanted. This is not just about material things, but that is a part of it. That's hard to admit; but it's true. It's also true that Jarrod is a great lover and he makes me laugh. I believe that we will make a dynamite couple. Whether it's right or not, my marriage to Chuck is over.

The Pursuer-Distancer Dance: The Woman's Perspective

We stated earlier our observation that, in growing numbers, high-powered women are distancing in their intimate relationships. To understand the reason this might be happening more these days than ever before, we must remember that people distance when under stress of a sort that stirs primitive-level discomforts. Men distance when they feel shamed by their subpar performance in their relationships or in the hunt—or when they are ashamed of how soothed they feel to be out of the hunt and in the arms of a nurturing woman.

Paralleling the male's shame regarding performance and closeness is the female's shame about not being comfortable enough in her role as nurturer. This struggle takes several forms.

Some women have difficulty compartmentalizing in the ways men can. Instinctively, men feel that working hard is the natural thing to do and that returning home to the open arms of a nurturing partner should naturally follow. Especially if their work is going well, they are able to put that hunter stuff in its own compartment and switch into readiness for connection.

But a woman's lengthy forays into the hunt are counter to her most gut-level pull to stay connected with loved ones. To endure, she goes numb. When she returns home after spending time in a man's world, what she brings with her is the same thing a man does: the need to be nurtured. But what she is met with is a man in need of the same thing: he, too, is in need of a nurturer.

What happens next puts women at a disadvantage. On a gut level, men feel justified in their frustrations with their exhausted mates; women feel ashamed that they are too exhausted to nurture. They may look or act like driven women who are just angry about the neediness of their sexist husbands. But their defensiveness comes from their own exhaustion that leaves them too far out of the position that is instinctively soothing to them: the role of nurturer.

A variant of this drama happens when the stress of being a super-nurturer depletes a woman, stress that is often fueled by her conflict over *not* being in the hunt. Remember that we do not limit our definition of high powered to hard-driving people pursuing careers; we work with many high-powered housewives. Often, these women are struggling in their role as nurturers. Their struggle comes from a drama that did not plague their ancestors: They feel almost as pulled to do their fair share of hunting as to be nurturers. When such a woman drops out of the hunt and assumes the role of nurturer, she is at risk of justifying her existence by driving herself with perfectionistic demands that eventually drain her. She drives herself and her loved ones. By the time he arrives home from the hunt, she distances because she's depleted and tired of feeding everyone and because he represents the reason that she is not fulfilling her need to do a fair share of hunting herself.

Shame over being good enough or comfortable enough in the role of nurturer propels women into distancing. The relationship then begins a downward spiraling. The more she distances, the less nurturing she acts, and the more she is confronted with not living up to the womanly role she is supposed to assume. The more tensions mount in the relationship, the more she distances.

Both of these distancing scenarios explain why so many women come alive when they are taken away from it all by a creative man who orchestrates a romantic interlude. We often hear our female clients relate some version of what we call *the wish:*

> I want my husband to just make it happen; kidnap me! Don't ask me to plan it. Just do it! If I have to plan it, it forces me to confront my own mixed feelings: Are the kids going to be okay while we're gone? Who's going to be there in case this or that goes wrong? Do I deserve to play? Do I still remember how to play? Once I run through all of the questions, I end up paralyzed.
>
> But if he just swoops me up—tells me we're going out to dinner, and ends up taking me off to the mountains for the weekend—then I feel as though he's created this safe little compartment in which he and I can play.

Wise men pay attention to the wish and make it their business to understand what it takes to create that feeling of safe play for their wives. When they do, the pursuer-distancer struggles in the relationship lessen. The trick is to learn what it takes to cover *her* bases, to defer to her notions about what needs to be in place at home for her to relax. In the same way that he may believe that he has better instincts about the hunt, she believes she has better instincts about the cave. Whether either actually does or doesn't is irrelevant; the question is what do my partner's instincts dictate, and what can I do to soothe her?

One couple we worked with had a diabetic child. Anxiety over this child's health paralyzed the wife and drained her. As their romance dwindled and conflict escalated, the couple considered divorce. His reasoning: "She's just not interested in me anymore. We haven't even been away alone for an overnight since our son was diagnosed, and that was over four years ago. I think that worrying about him is just an excuse to avoid me."

In response to our explanation of the wish, this man got creative. He arranged for a weekend stay in a romantic mountain setting just 90 miles from home. (In case they had to return to attend to their son, they could get there quickly.) He hired a baby-sitter whom he knew his wife trusted. And, solely in deference to his wife's anxieties, he also hired a temporary nurse to be on call the entire weekend in case the baby-sitter had any concerns about the son's diabetes. His reasoning: "Paying that nurse was a lot cheaper than paying for six more marital therapy sessions!"

When he kidnapped his wife and explained the arrangements he had made, every one of her fears about what would happen if she dared relax and play melted away. Their getaway weekend was the start of a long journey back into romance; it at least momentarily disrupted their pursuing and distancing.

Dilemmas for the Men Who Love Superachieving Women

The solution to most relationship problems used to be clear: get those men to slow down and learn to nurture. How things have changed! Today's men offer their own set of observations about the women they are trying to love.

Why Can't I Be Like Her?

An essay in *Fortune* magazine made the point that the first generation of women to become successful in corporate America is coming of age and confronting the kinds of midlife crises their fathers and grandfathers experienced. The authors pointed out that women now know what men have known all along: that work is hard; work takes a lot of time; work isn't always a day at the beach.

The *Fortune* article reported on a survey of 300 female managers and executives, ages 35 to 49. All but 13 percent had made or were seriously considering making a major change in their lives, and approximately one-third said they frequently felt depressed and trapped. More than half of these women had friends or colleagues who were getting a divorce or seeking therapy. The majority said they didn't have enough of a personal life and that much of their dissatisfaction stemmed from work.

So what are these women doing about this dilemma? They are blazing out of corporate America with as much force as they blazed trails into boardrooms during the prior two decades. Proclaiming more boredom than burnout; more of a revamping of their ideas of success than collision with a glass ceiling or a maternal wall, many of today's high-powered women are refusing to follow the masculine role models in which you struggle through a joyless, workaholic existence. Even the most ambitious of the women surveyed by *Fortune* indicated that they "were raised to expect their lives to be multidimensional, to include some combination of family, community, and outside interests."

But these corporate refugees also refuse to follow the female role models of the prior generation; they are *not* quitting their lucrative jobs to return home and have babies and bake cookies. Their sense of power bolstered by what they've accomplished, more than 90 percent of these women leave to create or join companies that allow them a more comfortable balance in their lives. A female marketing executive for American Express phrased it this way: "Our fire is in different places. We have the fire, but it is not necessarily directed at power and control."

Such changes seem to indicate a move toward a higher level of health for many women. However, what is not so often addressed is the effect that these changes are having in their marriages. There is little doubt that, as a group, men are envious of the freedom they perceive many women to have.

A focus group conducted for *Fortune* by Yankelovich Partners found that while men are compassionate about their wives redoing their careers to create more balance, their self-image as breadwinners responsible for the well-being of their families has snuffed out any serious consideration of making such changes themselves. One man put it this way: "Men have responsibilities, and women have choices." Asked how their wives would react if they announced they were having a midlife career crisis, most expressed the sentiment captured by one man's response: "Mine would say, 'Are you out of your mind? Get back to work.'"

What If She Won't Get a Job?

Seventy percent of wives of male executives (vice presidents and above) do *not* hold wage-earning jobs outside the home. Most often, this arrangement suits both spouses just fine. Most marriages that revolve around the careers of high-powered, executive-level males depend on a traditional marital arrangement in which having a wife to tend to family responsibilities frees the husband to devote the bulk of his time and energy to work.

Given that family life is also important to most of these men, they tend to appreciate their mate's willingness to assume the role of caretaker. "Knowing that my wife is there, overseeing things at home and taking care of my kids, allows me to concentrate on what I have to do," explained Jerry, a senior vice president in one of the largest banks in America. "If it weren't for my wife's willingness to stay at home, I can guarantee you I wouldn't be where I am in my career. I simply would not have been able to or willing to leave my kids alone."

We find that many men are not so compassionate and nurturing about this issue. Witness this conversation with a San Francisco cabbie:

Here I am, working six, usually seven days a week, twelve-to-fourteen hours every day, while my wife stays home trying to decide what she wants to do next. She used to make over one hundred grand a year in her own catering business. But she got tired of all of that. So she just quit!

I make good money, I'm not complaining about that. But I keep trying to tell her, "If you would just get a job in sales or something—you can sell anything with your personality and smarts—you would be pulling in some big bucks. And, with my flexible schedule, we could take some trips; have some weekends together. Make a marriage for God's sake!"

All she does is cry about it. All I do is get angry. She's a great person, but I'm not going to keep living like this. Why should I work like this when she won't do her share?

The Power of Her Resentments

What happens when a high-powered woman drives herself and her family too intensely for too long? The laments of Susan's husband, Harry, shed light on this dilemma.

> I'm tired of Susan's suffering. I know that I'm not being politically correct here, but I don't care; I'm beyond worrying about it.
>
> It's not that I don't appreciate all that she does. I simply am tired of hearing and seeing her struggle through her life. She wants more than she can have. She wants her career, but she also wants to be a hands-on manager of our household and parent to our kids. She also wants what only money can buy, a lot of money! Of course, she denies that this is true. She doesn't call it affluence or materialism. She just insists that we send our kids to private schools, that we take at least one nice vacation a year, that we have season tickets to the ballet, and on, and on, and on.
>
> It's not enough for us to work hard and make it to as many of our kids' activities as is *reasonable;* if we both don't attend everything, she wallows in guilt, turns it into anger, and spreads it all over me.
>
> It's not enough for us to exercise a *reasonable* amount, just to keep active. If she doesn't do her specified number of specific workouts, she's miserable, turns it into anger, and spreads it all over me.
>
> It's not enough for my kids to be kids. They have to perform up to her unbelievable standards. If they don't, she feels guilty about herself as a mother, angry with them for making her feel that way, and spreads that anger all over me.
>
> Our life saps us; we don't enjoy it. I'm sick and tired of her struggling and her anger.

Susan sat in stunned silence, her husband's words ringing in our office. From her perspective, her life had become a marathon of taking care of others: the needs of her customers, her work supervisors, her children, and her husband. And now she was being told that her way of driving herself was ruining the core of her life: her family relationships.

What happened next in our office was sadly predictable. Susan regrouped from her shock, regathered herself, and assumed a self-righteous stance. She began to assert the power of her resentments.

> If you attended to these children more, I would be less preoccupied with them. Tell me: What is the name of Karen's teacher? When is her first library project due? When is John's next dental appointment?
>
> You sit there and dare to criticize me about exercising? How much do you weigh now, compared to when we first met? You want to see the pictures? I squeeze out a few hours each week to take care of myself, and you dare to criticize me?
>
> I've told you ten thousand times, I'm not your mother. I don't have the luxury of staying home and letting my big strong man take care of me. You think we can live off your salary, even if we change the kids' school, sell our house, and do all those other fictitious things that we both know neither of us would tolerate doing?

Stinging from the shaming that his wife administered, Harry fell silent. For the remainder of our session, he gave one-word responses. He cancelled their next marriage counseling appointment, and we never heard from them again.

Fathering, Mothering, and Struggling

Even couples who openly appreciate their teamwork are apt to struggle with power issues. As the comments of Tina's husband, Tom, show, one such struggle is over parenting.

> When we were first married, it was clear that Tina was a lot more psychologically minded than I was. She is from a family that communicates, hugs, tolerates each other's differences—they're too good to be true.

> I, on the other hand, was from the proverbial big-boys-don't-cry-or-talk-about-it script. When we married, I knew so much less than Tina about how to be in a family.
>
> But we've been together for 14 years now, and I've done my work. I've agonized over the way I want to be; I've learned from my mistakes; I've read and paid attention; and I've become a different person.
>
> Problem is, Tina seems stuck in the notion that she will always be the primary parent in our family. I think that it's a competitive thing with her. Beyond the who-spends-the-most-time-with-the-kids issue, there is the matter of whose opinion counts most. Clearly, she believes that her way of parenting is better than mine.
>
> I've finally come to grips with the fact that being a good father is not the same as being a half-baked imitation of a good mother. But my struggle is with Tina. She just won't give ground on this I'm-the-family-mental-health-expert stuff.

Tom's comments portend struggles about more than parenting. In a backlash to the sensitive male phenomenon that emerged in reaction to feminism, more men today are proclaiming that they don't want to be women when they grow up; they are rejecting the notion that higher-order mental health is the same as disavowing their masculinity in favor of expressing their more feminine side. Some, like Tom, give voice to this sentiment by asserting themselves in appropriate ways. Others simply criticize their women.

Pleasing Others: Even If It Kills Them or Her

According to Harold,

> I wouldn't trade places with my wife for all the money in the world. She is constantly either anxious, sad, or angry about what she is not doing. She's never fully present. If she's out with me, she worries

about whether she spent enough time with the kids this week. If we do a string of family things, she decides that she and I don't have enough intimacy in our marriage. If she's working, she wants to be home. If she's home, she worries about work. You know the drill.

What I don't understand anymore is what this is all about. I thought that working hard together was supposed to create some sort of balance that we both enjoyed. Well, she got the first part right: the working hard part. That's all she does: she works at everything. But there's no balance.

In Bed with a Hunter-Woman: Whatever Happened to My Nurturing Wife?

A painful equivalent to criticizing a man for being a lousy hunter is accusing a woman of being a poor nurturer or a lousy lover. Such criticism hits her gut-level fear: "Maybe I can't really pull this off, being a powerful person and a good woman all at once."

Here, criticisms come in various guises. Some, like Jim's, focus on sexual dissatisfactions.

> Amy's too goal-directed about our sex life. I love the fact that we have discovered the fine and fun art of the quickie. But, I swear, I believe that this has become her first choice. She is always either too tired or too preoccupied to just relax and play for a while.

Others, like Max's, embed sexual complaints in broader dissatisfactions.

> Our sex life always comes up when I try to talk about the ways I'd like to change things between us. That's because I do wish we had more fun in bed. But Molly turns my message into a parody, and my point gets lost.
>
> Yes, I want more and better sex with her, but I also—and I *mainly*—want what would come before and after more and better sex: more fun and connection.

I'm lonely in this marriage. We have a business arrangement more than a romance. Three years ago she resigned from being the *family caretaker*, as she called it. She announced that she was tired of feeling the burden of responsibility for all of us, that she had lost her own identity, and that it was now time for us—meaning me—to take up some of our own slack.

Okay. So that means I do my own laundry and stuff like that. That's no big deal. But what is a big deal is her seeming not to notice me anymore. I came home from a three-day trip last week and she barely looked up from her book to greet me. It's not that she was cold; she just wasn't warm. As I said before, I'm lonely in this marriage.

People in these marriages sometimes go through an interesting twist on the old midlife crisis stereotype. Here, men don't run off in chase of younger women as a means of escaping anxiety about aging. Rather, most of the men we counsel who are having affairs are involved with women who are more nurturing and available than their mates, not more sexy or youthful. In fact, men often claim that sex in their affairs is not as good as sex with their spouses. What is *better* in their affairs than in their marriages are partners who are more nurturing, accepting, and available for emotional validation and connection. Their wives are stuck in vital exhaustion, bitterness, and passive or active criticism of them. The new partners are playful, accepting, and affirming—like a breath of fresh air to someone having difficulty breathing.

Nothing stirs anxieties about our ability to perform up to snuff more than a long-term relationship. As Dr. David Schnarch so eloquently explained it, a marriage serves as a crucible—a container that is dense enough to hold elements (a husband and a wife) while extraordinary heat (the stress of the Big Life) leads to a melding interaction that distills out the essences of each other. How you react once the heat starts soaring determines the quality of your relationship.

Chapter Six

Two Jobs, Two Kids, Too Much—
Parenting on Autopilot

In addition to struggling with their own relationships, many of today's Dynamic Duos also confront the complex issues of parenting. The first issue is whether there is room in the Dynamic Duo's lives for parenting. Next comes the question of the effects of the Dynamic Duo's lifestyle on the children.

Is There Room in Your Life for Parenting?

Is it possible to have a Big Life and raise a healthy family? Few questions stir as much passionate debate and late-night anxieties.

On the one hand, many lament that the blur of action that fills most households today keeps us from having healthy family relationships. Our lives are constant negotiations through a maze of chores. We carpool, arrange schedules, clean, shop, all the while working full- or part-time. As individuals, we feel violated by other family members' needs and demands as well as by our own stresses. Far too often, we take this sense of violation out on each other or ourselves.

Indeed, the Big Life leaves a shrinking amount of time and energy for parenting. A 1993 survey by the Family and Work Institute in New York found that parents of children under 18 spend only 3.2 hours in the presence of their children on workdays and 8.17 hours on days off. Approximately 12 percent of parents report that they either never have their main meal with their children or do so once a week or less.

Whether traditional activities like family meals are necessary to raise healthy families is a point of debate. It is clear, though, that when such rituals are absent, parents worry about whether their lives allow adequate room for raising a good enough family.

Special Considerations for Women

As of 1990, 74 percent of women between the ages of 20 and 44 were employed. Most of these women decided to become mothers. As of 1985, over 65 percent of mothers of school-age children in America were employed outside the home. As of 1992, 53 percent of women with infants were working outside the home, compared to only 38 percent in 1980. Nearly 77 percent of mothers of children age 18 or younger now work outside the home.

Mothers who work face soul-splitting challenges that give women considering motherhood reason to pause. In their groundbreaking book *Women and the Work/Family Dilemma*, Deborah Swiss and Judith Walker report on their study of 902 female graduates of Harvard's law, medical, and business schools. The authors found that some professional women were so wed to their jobs that they scheduled their children's births for a Friday so they could return to work on Monday. No wonder the authors only half-jokingly conclude that contemporary professional women only get to pick two of the following: family, career, or sanity.

If you are a career-minded woman, you may face a difficult choice between pursuing career excellence and becoming a mother. Gene Landrum, author of *Profiles of Female Genius—Thirteen Creative Women Who Changed the World*, notes that for one reason or another, really successful women often choose not to have children. Korn/Ferry International and UCLA's Anderson Graduate School of Management surveyed executive women in 1993 and found that 37 percent of the 439 respondents did not have children, compared with 5 percent of the executive men polled in a similar survey three years earlier.

For some women, not having children seems to happen by oversight. The climb up the career ladder becomes all-consuming, and decisions about marriage and family get constantly delayed. "While it became common knowledge that this generation of women could have babies well into their 40s, there was little talk of how difficult it could get after the age of 35."

These facts suggest that the decision to become a mother is virtually guaranteed to alter a woman's career path in ways that do not apply to men. Fair or not, this still seems to be the reality in today's world.

Special Considerations for High-Powered Men

It is a great fallacy that once the kids come, the overworked man will create a more balanced life. In truth, once they become fathers, most men work longer.

Contrary to what might seem obvious, it's not a desire to stay away from those dirty diapers and that exhausted wife that drives most new fathers further into the world of work. For many this is a necessity born of the fact that along with the babies comes their wives' withdrawal from wage earning. For others, increased work comes from more primitive urgings. In tandem with the stirring of a woman's nesting instincts on becoming a mother, men, once they become fathers, are stirred to sharpen their stick and intensify their hunting.

A 1993 *Time* magazine article pointed out that most career-minded men learn that advancement in their company will be seriously hindered if they defer to family life over the hard-driving, self-sacrificing work ethic. A 1989 survey of medium and large private employers found that only one percent of employees had the option of paid paternity leave and just 18 percent could take unpaid paternity leave. Even when such leave is available, only about seven percent of men working in large corporations take advantage of it.

The Take-Home Message

In deciding whether to have children and in adjusting to parenthood once the kids start to arrive, it is crucial that couples be realistic about what they will each face. Both at work and in their hearts, men and women experience different challenges: becoming a father pushes most men into the work world; becoming a mother propels most women into assuming an even larger caretaking role at home.

How Is the Big Life Affecting Our Children?

What is our lifestyle doing to our children? This is probably the most prevalent fear haunting today's families. Nearly 20 years ago, child expert David Elkind cautioned about the *hurried child syndrome*:

> Hurried children grow up too fast, pushed in their early years toward many different types of achievements and exposed to experiences that tax their adaptive capacity. . . . Hurried children are stressed by the fear of failure—of not achieving fast enough or high enough.

Hurried children are forced to take on the physical, psychological, and social trappings of adulthood before they are prepared to deal with them. We . . . dress our children in miniature adult costumes (often with designer labels), we expose them to gratuitous sex and violence, and we expect them to cope with an increasingly bewildering social environment. . . . Through all of these pressures the child senses that it is important for him or her to cope without admitting the confusion and pain that accompany such changes. Like adults, they are made to feel they must be survivors, and surviving means adjusting—even if the survivor is only four or six or eight years old. This pressure to cope without cracking is a stress in itself, the effects of which must be tallied with all the other effects of hurrying our children.

Why do we do this? According to Dr. Elkind, "By hurrying our children to grow up, or by treating them as adults, we hope to remove a portion of our burden of worry and anxiety and to enlist our children's aid in carrying life's load."

The list of various ways we hurry our children in deference to our own needs is sobering:

- *The child serves as a status symbol:*   Parents who feel conflict about staying home to serve as caretakers find justification in this role if their children bring enough attention and respect.
- *The child represents a surrogate self:*   Parents who are frustrated with competitiveness in the workplace soothe themselves by focusing on their children's accomplishments.
- *The child becomes the therapist:*   Parents who treat their children as confidants by telling them about their own personal lives—their feelings about the opposite sex or the child's other parent, for example—hurry them to grow up.
- *The child as a conscience:*   Parents sometimes turn to their children to understand and condone behavior that they, themselves, are in

conflict about. Examples include having a live-in sexual partner other than the child's other parent; absences from the child's extracurricular activities; substance abuse; or work addiction.

- *The child becomes the parents' partner:*   Parents entrap their children in a version of hurry sickness beginning at infancy, when children's instinctive sense of time flow may collide with parents' busy schedules. Children's daily lives are run by schedules imposed by day care, school, peer pressures, or various accommodations required by their parents' own Big Lives. As children adjust to all of this, they are taught to go numb and endure, not complain.

You May Reap What You Are Sowing

Virginia Price, one of the foremost authorities on Type A behavior pattern, cautioned that hard-driving, competitive, Type A people tend to parent in ways that foster similar reactions in their children:

- They react to children's behavior more often with criticism than with nurturing and praise.
- They perceive children as stressors because children lack skills needed to communicate and cope effectively.
- Their parental approval is contingent on the children performing in an exceptional manner in realms parents deem important.
- They attend primarily to the outcome and not to the process of their children's efforts.
- They severely criticize their children for behavior that does not meet parental expectations.
- They drive their children with messages to "hurry up," "be perfect," and "get more aggressive."
- They consistently model Type A behavior in the home.

Bearing in mind that children learn both from how they are treated as well as from what they observe, consider what your behavior teaches your children:

If children see parents living in states of constant readiness, prepared for something to happen, they learn to be hypervigilant.

If children see parents always on the alert for hidden challenges when dealing with others, they will grow up thinking such behavior is completely appropriate, even necessary.

If children see parents constantly struggling against time and other people, they will learn that life is a struggle.

If children see parents constantly setting excessively high performance standards for themselves, rejoicing only when their achievements are recognized by others and reproaching themselves when they fail to meet their perfectionistic standards, they will grow up to exhibit these same characteristics.

Indeed, Type A behavior pattern can be detected in children as young as age four. If we listen closely, we will hear complaints from our children that can serve as mirrors to our own behavior.

What Children Say about Their High-Powered Fathers

A study of executives' children found that their biggest complaint was their fathers' rigid, nonnegotiable demands for compliance with their own points of view and their lack of effort to understand the children's views. Other studies of adolescents have shown that they are especially likely to shy away from discussing important issues with their fathers when the fathers' helping style was to lecture them; influence them with facts, arguments, and logic; order or command them to do something; and criticize or blame them.

This may not be news for many of us. The struggles between high-powered, overbearing fathers and their children—especially their adolescents—is the stuff that movies and stereotypes are made of. What is far more surprising to most people is the information that follows.

What Children Say about Their High-Powered Mothers

A high-powered woman who decides to focus on child rearing is at significant risk of overly stressing her children with her own perfectionistic standards. Virginia Price cautions that, because they are "her most important achievement," a high-powered mother may be reluctant to encourage, or even allow, her youngsters to develop self-reliant behaviors, since to become independent may involve their making choices that are not in harmony with her's. The risks here are considerable.

- Mothers who are dominating, controlling authorities may produce children who are excessively dependent on approval for their sense of well-being. In this way—contrary to the popular mythology that it is hard-driving fathers who shape Type A behavior in children—many mothers play a dominant role in passing on high-powered coping patterns to their offspring.
- Children who are treated as if their worth lies in doing exactly as they are told, behaving perfectly, and achieving outstanding success learn to doubt themselves unless they are performing up to another's standards. They learn to tie their personal worth to these behaviors.
- Observations of interactions between Type A boys and their mothers reveal that these mothers habitually escalate the performance standards of their sons. Some research suggests that Type A behavior originates in families having an aggressive, demanding mother and a psychologically passive or absent father.

A high-powered woman may also perceive family turmoil as a challenge requiring her special caretaking skills. If she takes on the job of minimizing conflicts among other family members, she may settle into a life at the apex of communication triangles formed by other loved ones who do not deal directly or effectively with each other. This pattern carries both high risks and valued rewards to such women. The consequences include chronic stress, frustration with loved ones, and eventual emotional exhaustion. Yet, being the hub of the wheel in the family setting may also be a power position. "The sense of control derived from being the central person in the family may seem well worth the problems entailed."

Superachieving Children

Dr. Karen Matthews of the University of Pittsburgh is one of our country's leading health psychologists. She cautions that contemporary lifestyles often lead to superachieving Type A behaviors in children. Her research suggests that teachers' ratings of factors such as those below are diagnostic of Type A behavior in children:

1. Competitiveness
2. Work style: quick and energetic rather than slow and deliberate
3. Impatience when forced to wait for others
4. Impatience when forced to work with slower children
5. Tendency to do things in a hurry
6. How easily they become angry or irritated at peers
7. Tendency to interrupt others
8. Level of leadership in various activities
9. Argumentitiveness
10. Restlessness when forced to sit still for long periods
11. Winning seems to be more important than having fun in games or schoolwork
12. Tendency to get into fights

We are not encouraging you to label your child. Neither do we intend to add to that bagful of parenting guilt that most of us carry around. As you will see in the following, the presence of hard-driving characteristics during childhood does not necessarily indicate a problem. Our point is simply to encourage you to notice that your children are not immune to the effects of the Big Life.

Noticing how your children cope leads to the logical question—where do these tendencies come from? Parents are certainly not the only influence shaping a child's behavior or stress levels. In many instances, parents aren't even the major factors influencing children, especially once they enter early adolescence. In addition to family, children are impacted by their schools, the media, peers, and the consequences of their actions. It also seems that some people are born with a temperament that predisposes them to cope in certain ways.

We remind you that high-powered coping is not a bad thing; it is not a sign of maladjustment or of any character defect. In fact, just as with adults, some children who show high-powered traits thrive. Compared to others, superachieving children have been found to be brighter, more physically fit, more talkative, outgoing, and socially skilled. Furthermore, many children outgrow Type A behavior. Children who show Type A behavior do not necessarily grow up to be Type A adults. If Type A behavior is still present at adolescence, however, the likelihood is far greater that this style of coping will be carried into adulthood.

What Children Do to High-Powered Parents

Relationships always operate like a circle. *A* influences *B*, and *B* influences *A*. This is perhaps nowhere more evident than in relationships between parents and their children. Children can have a substantial impact on parents, increasing stress and anger and often producing a struggle for control that can be particularly toxic for high-powered parents who are accustomed to being in charge.

Parenting may also reactivate conflicts from parents' own childhoods. This was the case for Louis, who sought our help to better understand why he felt so ill at ease whenever he was left alone with his children. After several sessions spent exploring his own first family experiences, the source of his uneasiness became clear.

> Saturday was my favorite day when I was a kid, not just because I got a day off from school; but that was grilling-out day in my family. My father and I had a routine: Around 11 o'clock on Saturday morning, he lit the charcoal, and while the barbecue pit was heating and the hamburgers were cooking, he and I played catch. I remember wishing that the charcoal would cool down and not cook so fast. As soon as the burgers were cooked, our game of catch ended.
>
> After we ate lunch, my dad turned on the TV, and we watched whatever ball game came on. My dad always fell asleep about 30 minutes into the game. Then that was it. I'd go my way, and he'd sleep the rest of the afternoon.
>
> I loved those minutes with my dad. He basically ignored me the rest of the time.
>
> Now I find myself operating with that same kind of internal clock that used to be ticking during our games of catch. After I'm with my kids for just a little while, I get squirmy. Until now, I never knew where that anxiety came from; it never made sense to me. The truth is that I love spending time with my kids, especially now that they are a little older. But I still feel as though those hamburgers are going to be cooked too soon, and the alarm for disconnecting from my family is about to ring.

Parenting forces us to test the limits of our own ineptness. Whatever conflicts we struggle with will be pushed and tested by the stress of parenting. For high-powered men, this often means that uncomfortable feelings and conflicts about attachment versus productivity get roused by time spent parenting. For high-powered women, conflicts about giving a good enough amount of nurturing and struggles over caretaking versus self-care come with motherhood.

Helping the Next Generation

The following questions point out what we need to manage to parent in ways that help ourselves and our children:

- How often do your children see you relaxed and playful compared to stressed, exhausted, or angry?
- Are your kids better off with fewer activities and calmer parents?
- Do you teach your children to fear wasting time?
- Do you maintain contact with your children by keeping up with who they know, what they do, what they like, and what they worry about?
- Are you creating family rituals that teach children to protect time for loved ones, even in a busy life?
- Are you teaching your children to be loyal to loved ones?
- Are you honest about the effects that your life is having on your children?
- Are you doing your fair share of parenting scutt work? This last point deserves elaboration.

The Benefits of the Scut Work

Psychologist Ron Taffel noted that the parent who participates in what he termed *the daily scut work with kids* will be the parent who develops a relationship with them. Children operate on their own schedule of when and how they communicate, and only a person who spends time carpooling, hanging out, and otherwise being in their vicinity will discover what they think, need, and feel.

This creates a dilemma for high-powered, busy parents. If we are particularly well-intended, we might schedule quality time with our kids. But our notions of when and how to connect do not always jibe with our children's internal time clocks. It's important not to discount the wisdom of continuing to pursue connection, even when our efforts do not seem to be paying off.

It is crucial that we not discount the importance of our mere presence to our children or the effects that our lifestyle choices have on them. Through our divorces, stress, or work, most of us disconnect from our kids. They and we then suffer. Most of us caught in the Big Life need to mindfully work to make time to spend with our children; otherwise, it just won't happen. We need to regularly join them in their world and, where possible, invite them into ours.

We need also to be realistic. Realistic about whether we are willing to make room in our lives for parenting, and realistic about the effects that our lives are having on our children. We need to dispel the myth that children are very adaptable and will adjust easily to major changes or unrelenting stress, simply because their doing so is important to us.

No stress stirs us like parenting stress. Faced with any excessive stress, we reach for our ace-in-the-hole coping strategies, which often are fueled more by myths than by realistic notions about the ways men and women cope.

Chapter Seven

Twenty Myths about Supercouples (Why Xena and Hercules Have Lousy Love Lives)

In a chain reaction, your thinking affects your feelings which, in turn, affect the ways you cope and handle relationships. So managing yourself and your relationships starts with an examination of your thinking—or beliefs.

High-powered people are often driven by beliefs that discount themselves or others, create unrealistic expectations, or perpetuate self-soothing fantasies. In this chapter, we explore the 20 myths these beliefs create, and the truths that counter them.

MYTH 1: MY STRESS HURTS ME MORE (OR LESS) THAN YOURS HURTS YOU.

Two variants of this myth can complicate your life. In the first, mutual support is ruined by the suffering contest in your relationship. Requests for support are aborted by responses that one-up the original sufferer's pain. "You think *you* need a break? Let me tell you how *my* life has been going lately. *I'm* the one who's exhausted."

Just as frequently, we discount our own struggles. We accumulate a vague sense of shame about the impact that our Big Life is having on others, and this predisposes us to defer to others' struggles over our own. It's as if *their* stress is more important or painful than our own.

> Truth: Your life is not a suffering contest. Your stress is major to you, and no one else's stress is more or less noble or important.
>
> *So: Honor each other's struggles. Express appreciation for your partner without devaluing yourself. You can simultaneously nurture and solicit support.*

MYTH 2:   WORKING WHEN NO ONE IS LOOKING (OR AWAKE) WILL HAVE NO EFFECT ON MY RELATIONSHIPS.

This is a classic mistake made by the high powered. We convince ourselves that we need relief from our anxiety about our burgeoning to-do list more than we need rest or relaxation. As one of our clients put it: "I just figure that by getting up at 4:00 each morning I can get a jump on my day before my family wakes. That way no one loses. I get my work done and still get to spend a little time with them before leaving for the office."

> Truth: Working more may relieve anxiety, but it does not create energy. Periodically overworking doesn't hurt anyone. But if you don't control your own workaholic tendencies, you will lose your creativity and coping flexibility and drain energy from those around you. Family or work teams operate like systems: They organize around the most consistent patterns, and what happens to one member affects and is affected by the others. You have a limited amount of coping energy available in a given space of time (such as a week). Regardless of when you expend it, drained is drained.
>
> *So: Take the time to rest and relax. The most fundamental stress management tool is taking care of yourself.*

MYTH 3: EXPRESSING ANGER IS FAR BETTER THAN HOLDING IT IN.

Rushing through life without accumulating irritations and resentments is impossible. This is a given in the Big Life, but it does not have to be a problem. The question is what happens next. It is here that action-oriented, high-powered people tend to make a mistake: they believe that expressing anger is always the best course of action.

> Truth: Whether expressing anger is a healthy choice depends on *how* and *when* it is expressed. Behaving aggressively does nothing but hurt others and fuel your own hostility. You might feel temporary relief, but the long-range consequences of striking out at others leaves them damaged and you suffering the consequences of unchecked hostility. In either case, you lose.
>
> *So: Learn to be appropriately assertive, not aggressive, to effectively manage conflict. A good rule of thumb is to always act (not strike) when the iron is warm (not hot).*

MYTH 4: IF IT DOESN'T COME NATURALLY, THEN IT'S FRAUDULENT.

This myth squelches more personal and relationship growth than any other. Changing the way you cope or deal with others feels awkward. If you run from the awkwardness back into old-time behavior, your awkwardness leaves, but no change happens. This leads to unnecessary, self-limiting ways of managing ourselves.

> Truth: Most of the valuable things learned in life do not come naturally—they have to be practiced until they feel familiar. For most of us, changing involves progressing through the steps depicted below.

THE CHANGE PROCESS

Imagine it	→	*Pretend it*	→	*Become it*
Attitudinal change	→	Behavioral change	→	Emotional Change

First, *imagine* how you want to be. Clarify on an attitudinal (or conceptual) level the changes that you want to make, and then commit yourself to making these changes.

Next, practice *behaving* in harmony with your imagination. This often means tolerating the awkwardness that comes when you do something new. It is okay to pretend to be a certain way because you have decided that's the way you want to be.

Only after many practice trials (pretending) will a new way of acting begin to feel natural and authentic. At that point, an emotional change occurs; the imagined and pretended ways of acting start to feel natural and authentic.

So: Clarify conceptually how you want to be. Practice behaving that way, over and over again. Eventually, this new way of behaving becomes familiar and happens as second nature. Accept that the price you pay for changing is bearing through the awkwardness of changing. Learning to be a better listener, to slow down, to change health habits, to be more affectionate, to be a more creative lover, to better manage anger, to stop procrastinating—these and other desireable changes are not likely to come naturally, but they are attainable. If you can imagine it, you can pretend it. If you pretend it long enough, you become it.

The second half of this book describes a program to help you achieve change.

MYTH 5: IF I TAKE APPROPRIATE CARE OF MYSELF, I'LL BECOME LAZY.

Most high-powered people fear that if they slow down enough to thaw out from their stress-induced numbness, they'll never get going again. This fear is born of lack of experience. You probably have spent so little time appropriately pacing and nurturing yourself, that to do so feels awkward and unnatural.

Truth: After a period of rest or play, it often *is* difficult to once again get going. Evidence of this is the proverbial Sunday evening blues. Dreading the start of yet another exhausting week on the tail of a relaxing weekend, we drift into irritation and depression as our recess draws to a close. But don't be confused: It doesn't mean that you are a lazy person. It means that you are a tired person.

So: *Dare to see what happens to your productivity if you begin taking more appropriate care of yourself in small ways. Try exploring a different pace, a different style, a different set of choices in a given day.*

MYTH 6:   IF I DON'T SHOW STRENGTH, I'LL LOSE.

High-powered people often confuse staying distant in relationships with having power. They even adopt adages that justify this stance:

"Whoever has the information has the power."

Implication: *If you want to remain one-up in your struggle for power, don't share information.*

"If you aren't winning, you are losing."

Implication: *Don't compromise in a disagreement or negotiation. Dig in, even if it damages the relationship.*

"Power is an aphrodisiac."

Implication: *If you want to remain attractive to your partner, don't show vulnerability.*

This last adage particularly applies to men and women caught-up in the big-stick-gets-the-love mentality. Here, we overfocus on the hunt in a misguided effort to recapture, keep, or gain a partner's approval. Your partner wants a companion, but your work, fatigue, preoccupation, or irritation keeps you from each other. Your partner grows lonely because of your absences. The result? Rather than gain approval, you lose your attractiveness to your partner.

> Truth: Acting on this myth is a fundamental way that many high-powered people alienate themselves from others. Power, prestige, or position might make you attractive to a relatively new observer, but long-range growth in any relationship depends more on how you treat each other than on any other single factor. Lifelong intimacy grows out of affection, playfulness, and connection.
>
> *So: Pause and consider your partner's definition of powerful. Dare to ask your partner if your way of showing strength is attractive. Also dare to notice what effects you are generating in others. What do the responses of those around you suggest about the effects that your way of living has on them?*
>
> *Practice showing your humanness to others. On a daily basis, disclose to selected friends, associates, and loved ones certain vulnerabilities. Doing so will make you approachable, someone others can learn to trust. It also gives you support of the sort that helps you cope.*

MYTH 7:   APOLOGIZING SHOWS WEAKNESS.

Here is the proverbial syndrome: The Big Life speeds us up; in our hurry we step on others' toes, hurting and disappointing them and ourselves; we accumulate regrets, and tensions grow in our relationships. Fearing that we are losing our attractiveness (see Myth 6), we drift into silence, keep on pushing the Big Life, and our own and others' wounds remain unsoothed.

> Truth: The three most powerful words in any relationship are "I am sorry." Expressing regret over a conflict, mistake, or transgression doesn't lessen your clout, it increases the power of your influ-

ence in another person's life. When you apologize, others feel acknowledged and understood. They then lower their defenses, and further connection between you is possible.

So: Apologize generously. Regularly take an honest inventory of the effects you have had on others, and let them know that you apologize for any hurt or stress you may have caused them.

MYTH 8: WE CAN'T BE BUSY AND HAVE HEALTHY RELATIONSHIPS.

All-or-nothing thinking of this sort is what keeps many of us from doing those little things that create relationships and make them grow. The busier we get, the more we tend to idealize how comfortable our relationships would be *if only:* we had a less complicated life; we had more money and time; we lived like the people next door. To whom do you compare yourself in this regard?

Truth: There is no such thing as a perfect family or relationship. Even more important: There are no secret rules that define what has to be done for your family to stay healthy through all the stages of life together. Relationships are amazingly resilient: if they are regularly fed at least a little, they grow.

So: Do what is possible; it will add up and keep you connected. Take advantage of routine times that bring you together, such as carpooling or commuting. Turn off the radio or music in the car and talk and listen! Remember: there is no norm for today's family. Create your version of family, and feel good about it.

MYTH 9: THE SKILLS THAT MAKE ME SUCCESSFUL AT WORK WILL ALSO MAKE ME SUCCESSFUL AT HOME.

It's another classic mistake: The high-powered person tries to manage home life in the same style that succeeds so well at work. For the most part, attributes like commitment, honesty, perseverance, and willingness to delay gratification can serve you well in many spheres, including your relationships. But relationships require certain things to make them grow that cannot come from your work style.

Truth: Relationships grow from connection, not from performance or management. To connect you must slow down, attend, disclose yourself, and nurture.

So: *Post a sign in your house to remind you that "No superpeople live here!" Throughout the day, periodically shift gears out of your hurry sickness and high-powered flurries. Pause and notice the people in your life and show them that you respect their realities. Don't let your high-powered coping damage others.*

MYTH 10:   THE EFFICIENT WAY IS ALWAYS THE BETTER WAY.

In our chronic rushing, we learn to be efficient. What we don't learn is how to act when speed doesn't really matter. We get lulled into assuming that the moral high ground is gained by doing even mundane things with maximal efficiency. The result? We needlessly drive ourselves and others.

Truth: Driving yourself with an excessive need for efficiency does not lead to more time spent relaxing; it simply leads to more time spent stewing over whether you could have gotten through yet another moment of your life more quickly.

So: *Realistically analyze the costs and benefits of your style. Notice whether the price you pay for your efficiency is worth the outcomes you generate in relationships. For example, you might find yourself commenting as you enter a restaurant, "If you had*

*turned left on 53rd street as I told you, we would have gotten here
sooner."*
*Stop! Notice your partner's reaction—the look on his or her face; the
words said; the energy drain that comes from yet another of your criticisms. Now, calculate exactly how much time would have been saved
if your partner had done it your way, and especially take note of
whether it matters. Is satisfying your compulsion to control really
worth the price exacted from your relationship?*

MYTH 11:   WHOEVER GETS THERE FIRST WINS.

A variant of the efficiency myth is the belief that we win some secret
competition if we get wherever we are going or accomplish whatever we are pursuing *sooner than.* Sooner than *what* or *who* remains
unspecified. Rushing as a lifestyle is a natural outgrowth of the
hurry sickness we live in. Have you ever found yourself in a tense
race with the car next to you, just to earn the privilege of being the
first to stop at the next stop light?

> Truth: Most rushing comes from a blind acceptance of another's
> urgent agenda, which resulted from that person blindly accepting the
> urgency of someone else who made the same mistake by accepting
> yet another's urgency.
> So: *Practice pacing yourself. You've already proven to the world
> that you are a good sprinter. Now, adopt a new goal: Show that you
> can take charge of your own pace and style.*

MYTH 12:   WHEN DEALING WITH OTHERS, TAKE
ADVANTAGE OF EVERY TEACHABLE MOMENT.

High-powered types sometimes find it difficult not to share what
they know with others, especially when those others don't seem to

know what they are doing. After all, we often see a better way of doing things, and we just want to be helpful by sharing these insights. But these acts of help can backfire, as Bruce's story illustrates.

You know, my eight-year-old daughter, Kelly, just started playing soccer on the community team. She loves it! All she talks about is her soccer team. But she's not very coordinated, and she gets frustrated. I want to help her out, so I kick the ball around with her whenever we can.

Well, last Saturday we were in the back yard messing around with the ball, having what I thought was a great time. Ten minutes into it, Kelly looked up at me with that sweet face and said, "Daddy, how about if we just *play* for a little while; and maybe then you can teach me?"

I swear, her words hit me like a truck: Most of what I say to my baby is instructional. I constantly correct her. God knows, it's not because I'm critical of her; I'm her biggest fan! But I must be a pain for her sometimes. I never just let her be.

Truth: Often, being taught feels like being lectured, corrected, controlled, or criticized.

So: Be humble. Remind yourself that you are not the annointed "teacher of humanity." Practice biting your tongue. Decide once a week to mindfully listen to others rather than teach or preach. Reflect what you hear them saying or feeling. Offer encouragement, admiration, compassion, or support—but not advice. More frequently, let yourself and others just be.

MYTH 13:   I CAN'T HELP IT.

Most of us justify our inappropriate behavior with some combination of self-abdicating myths. We believe: "My genes made me do it!" Or, "My parents' past relationships made me this way." Or, "The environment is making me do it." Or "*You* are making me do it." Whatever the *it* might be—angry outbursts, workaholism, coldness, or compulsions—we justify staying the same, even if *it* is hurting us and others.

> Truth: Our most enduring power involves controlling what happens *next* in our lives. Regardless of the hand we're dealt, we have choice about how we cope.
>> So: *Stop blaming other people and circumstances for your actions. Remember that the question is not* why, *but* how. *Regardless of the reasons you cope as you do, ask how you might benefit from controlling your subsequent behaviors. Learn to disrupt your typical coping strategies that cause problems in your life.*

MYTH 14: IF MY PARTNER HELPED OUT ENOUGH, MY JUGGLING STRUGGLE WOULD GO AWAY.

Many high-powered people follow the motto suggested by a 74-year-old woman we knew: "When something goes wrong, find out who's to blame and blame that sucker!"

When we are overwhelmed, it's only natural to assume that there must be something that others could do to help. When that help doesn't happen, we conclude that our pain is due to *their* lack of cooperation. Soon, we lock-in to assumptions that damage our relationships: If my partner nurtured me more, my emptiness and fatigue would go away. Or, if the guy in the next office worked harder, my stress would go away.

> Truth: Stress is an unavoidable part of the Big Life; it doesn't necessarily mean that anyone is doing anything to you. Most often, our distress comes from not taking appropriate care of ourselves.
>> So: *Focus on controlling your own reactions when you are stressed, not on what others are or are not doing.*

MYTH 15:   BECAUSE TRYING HARDER THAN THE NEXT PERSON IS THE KEY TO MY SUCCESS, A GOOD GAUGE OF WHETHER I'VE HAD A GOOD DAY IS WHETHER I AM EXHAUSTED.

Do you work yourself to exhaustion by operating under the following beliefs?

THE ONLY WAY FOR ME TO:	IS TO:
Get nurtured	Be strong
Feel good enough	Be perfect
Feel that I deserve to rest and enjoy	Try harder
Be understood and accepted	Please others
Finish	Hurry
Feel safe	Be careful

Truth: Operating under these beliefs yields mixed blessings. On the one hand, these drivers will serve you well. On the other, blindly following their dictates will ruin the quality of your life, starting with your relationships.

This doesn't mean hard work is not necessary to be successful. But it is important to take note of where you are right now. You may have established your business by being the first to arrive and the last to leave your office each day. Today's question is whether that work style has become habit rather than a necessity.

So: *Experiment periodically with* not *trying harder than the next guy.*

MYTH 16:   BECAUSE MY MAIN JOB IS EARNING MY KEEP, I HAVE NO TIME FOR ENJOYMENT OR PLAY.

By early adulthood (if not sooner) most of us have internalized the messages in the myths outlined above. Now, we battle with an inner voice that is quieted only if we work. We get confused; we think that quieting this internal nagging regarding the dozens of tasks which have to be done is the same as relaxing.

Many of us have spent so many years producing that we have forgotten what it means to enjoy. We confuse aversion relief with pleasure. The endless items on our to-do lists make us anxious, and getting some of that stuff done lessens our anxiety. Some even decide that "getting work done is fun; it makes me feel good." Maybe so. But that's not the same as having fun; it's akin to what happens if you have a headache and it goes away: Not having the headache is a relief, but it isn't the same as feeling really great.

Does this apply to you? Have you internalized messages that interfere with your ability to enjoy? Find out if you know how to play by imagining or recalling yourself doing the activities described in the middle column, at the ages listed in the left-hand column below. Next, imagine or recall who reacted to you and how, when you were doing that activity.

AT AGE:	IF YOU WERE:	WHO REACTED HOW?
6 years	Running, playing, being rambunctious	_____
13	Playing ball; giggling with a friend	_____
17	Hanging out on a Saturday	_____
21	Taking the summer off to travel or to combine working with traveling	_____
25	Hanging out on a weekend	_____
35	Going to a ball game with buddies; taking a day off to shop and visit with friends	_____

AT AGE:	IF YOU WERE:	WHO REACTED HOW?
45	Taking a night off from work of any sort (home or office)	_____

Your descriptions in the right-hand column probably paint a clear picture: starting in late adolescence (if not sooner), the world told you "Get to work. Behave. Stop wasting time." Most of us internalize the message that we need to produce to earn our right to exist. Doing so means blocking certain natural tendencies and needs, such as being playful, saying no, slowing down, acting adventuresome, or showing curiosity. Because it's not okay to express these aspects of yourself, you split them off, suppress them, and behave instead in ways that are acceptable.

> Truth: In both relationships and work, the best antidote to burnout is engaging in pleasure and playfulness.
> *So: Force yourself to relearn what pleasure is. This takes practice. Start by doing more frequently the things that used to bring you pleasure, the stuff that made you squirm with anticipation.*

MYTH 17:   I'M NOT GOOD AT INTIMACY, SO I MIGHT AS WELL AVOID IT.

We spend most of our lives studying, working, achieving, and doing. We spend relatively little time playing, touching, communicating, or making love. The result? Intimacy becomes an area of relative inexperience and awkwardness for many high-powered people.

Some of us have felt the sting of criticism in these areas.

- A lonely, disgruntled partner complains about your long work hours.

- A sexually frustrated partner complains that your fatigue or your hurriedness makes you a lousy lover.
- The look of fear or anxiety in your children's eyes says that they don't know you or trust you as much as you wish they did.

For some, the problem isn't a lack of skill; it's a lack of comfort. Many high-powered men have lost their sense of masculinity because of the issues we discussed earlier in this book. Likewise, many high-powered women fear that they have lost their femininity. What happens next is what some believe to be inevitable—a loss of romance.

> Truth: Romance, nurturing, communication, and intimacy require energy. You can't exhaust yourself and remain an effective partner or lover.
>
> *So: Be generous and gracious. This is the best advice we have to offer couples. If we collapse all of the little things that add up to a relationship that works across the long run, these two factors emerge. Thriving partners treat each other with generosity. They regularly offer each other gifts that they know the other cherishes.*
>
> *And they react graciously to the gifts that are offered. Inside the bedroom and out, they don't complain about what they are given; they appreciate it, even if it is not their first choice.*

MYTH 18:   MY PRESENCE DOESN'T REALLY MATTER MUCH TO MY LOVED ONES, SO I MIGHT AS WELL ENDURE LONG PERIODS OF ABSENCE FROM THEM.

Busy people sometimes justify doing what they love rather than being with those they love. But this is not always as it appears.

If you believe that your value lies in what you can produce, you are likely to assume that your mere presence doesn't really matter to the people you love. And given how busy our loved ones are, it is easy to get confused about whether our presence in their lives is a burden or a blessing.

Truth: If you listen and watch closely, you will see the fallacy in this way of thinking. Who are the teachers? Out of the mouths of babes comes the truth.

Sarah, an international travel consultant, tried to soothe her seven-year-old daughter's sadness about her upcoming nine-day business trip. "I have to go, Sweetie; it's business. Plus, I will make a bunch of money from this trip. But when I get home, I'll be here to stay for the rest of the month. We'll go to the zoo and have time to do all sorts of things together." The daughter (with tears): "I don't want to go to the zoo; I want to be with you."

So: *Connect repeatedly and in various ways with the people you love, even when they are not particularly responsive. This is the way to keep love alive.*

MYTH 19:   WHAT I WANT IS NOT AS IMPORTANT AS WHAT OTHERS NEED.

This myth leads us to not assert and nurture ourselves. We fail to set appropriate limits and end up feeling misunderstood and invaded. This happens in various ways:

- We repeatedly respond to others' urgency at the expense of our own needs, and our frustrations build.
- Because we discount the caring or competence of others, we habitually stay quiet about our own needs. Rather than letting others know what we think, feel, need, or want, we become experts at simply going numb and keeping on going.

The result? Feelings of abuse, loneliness, being taken advantage of, and being unloved accumulate. Next, we either explode or launch into the world of work and things and projects to distract ourselves from the accumulated tensions in the world of people.

Truth: You cannot be effective in relationships until you learn to nurture yourself; and to the extent that you do not take care of yourself, you will struggle in relationships. Avoiding this pitfall involves fundamental choices, each of which seems inconsequential in the moment.

So: *Notice the small stuff. For example, pause and decide what you would really like to eat for lunch; don't just gobble something based on routine or convenience.*

At least once each day, say no to some request for your time or energy. Instead of filling that time with another obligation, do something that is a healthy pleasure for you. In small ways, finish unfinished business with associates and loved ones.

MYTH 20: I WILL CONTINUE TO BE AN EXCEPTION TO THE RULES.

As we zoom through the Big Life, we accumulate evidence supporting this myth. After all, we do prove to be the exception to many rules. We often are able to do more than others, accumulate more than others, or endure more than others. But experience has a way of equalizing us.

Truth: No one is the exception to certain rules regarding the human condition and the workings of relationships. No matter how stress-hardy it might be, if you don't nurture the relationship, it will wither.

So: *Be humble; accept the fact that you are not the exception to the rules. Honestly evaluate yourself: How are you living; what effects do you have on others; and what might you do to take better care of yourself and your relationships.*

The latter half of this book shows you exactly how to organize your efforts to *BEat Stress Together.*

Chapter Eight

How to Beat Stress Together

As the first half of this book makes clear, today's no-time supercouples are under constant pressure—at work and at home. But harried supercouples can become satisfied Dynamic Duos through *BE*ating *S*tress *T*ogether (BEST). The remainder of this book will explain how doing your BEST can make your relationship better.

The nine components of BEST are:

- Recognizing stress reactions
- Learning to handle change
- Destressing your environment
- Building a life in harmony with your values
- Resolving role conflicts
- Finding (or making) time
- Overcoming hurry sickness
- Changing fantasies into action plans
- Renegotiating your relationship to keep intimacy alive

Regardless of the specific changes you want to make, if you are serious about developing a healthier and happier way of living, then you must commit yourself to practicing BEST. It will help you understand that much of your discontent comes from your struggling, not from your stress. It will also help expand your shopworn coping style so that you can preserve and enrich your relationships. The steps involved in BEST are not mystical. However, the effects of this process can be rather magical in improving the quality of your life and your relationships.

The first six components of the BEST program discussed in this chapter are the foundation for individual stress management. The final three components rounding out the BEST program go beyond traditional stress management by setting the entire stress management process in a relationship context. These three components are extensively discussed in the remaining chapters.

What Is Stress?

Stress occurs whenever people are faced with a need to adjust or cope. In other words, stress is what happens whenever we are awake.

Think about it: Your life is filled with demands to adapt to events, people, and environments. Some adjustments are major; most are relatively small. These demands stir a combination of psychological and physical reactions—the stress response.

What Is Your Body Telling You?

Imagine taking a nice, leisurely walk around your neighborhood on a beautiful spring day. You are relaxed and peaceful, enjoying the fresh air and the sights, sounds, and smells. Suddenly you hear growling and barking. An angry dog is near. In an instant a huge, black Doberman is running toward you with its teeth bared. How do you react? You might stay and fight—but if you are smart, you'll turn heel and run.

Fight or Run

The best way to understand stress reactions is to think of what happens whenever people are faced with an emergency like this. At such times, the body reflexively turns on its alarm reaction, called the *fight-or-flight syndrome.* This is the human version of overdrive.

First, the adrenal glands give the body a large squirt of adrenaline, which begins a series of adjustments that prepare us to deal with the emergency. The heart rate increases and pumps extra blood to the large muscles. At the same time, the peripheral vascular system—made up of the small veins and arteries near the surface of the skin—constricts. This allows less blood to circulate close to the skin's surface, an important phenomenon in the event of being cut during battle.

Once the emergency is dealt with, the parasympathetic nervous system kicks in and calms the fight-or-flight response. This response comes in handy in extreme circumstances—such as battling angry dogs. However, this response doesn't always serve us well in our day-to-day life. After all, life might get a little complicated if people started bolting from tense business meetings or punching out everyone who aggravates them. This leads to a fundamental stress management problem: Each day, the fight-or-flight response is turned on 20 to 40 times, but we seldom have the opportunity to turn it off.

If a superachiever's stress reaction were charted through a given day, the physical and emotional tension and fatigue levels would look like an upwardly moving stock market graph. Spikes corresponding with moments of fight-or-flight response would be followed by slight declines as the superachiever begins to calm down. But this calm is interrupted by another spike as the fight-or-flight reaction once again kicks into high gear. Gradually but progressively, stress levels elevate. This kind of ongoing stress has a cumulative wear-and-tear effect.

Momentary stress reactions do not typically hurt people. In fact, they help us to cope. But living day after day on an upwardly moving stress curve leads to both emotional and physical problems, including free-floating alarm. Constant arousal leaves us charged up with no particular focus. The chronic emergency reaction also leaves us tightly wound and ready to strike out at the next mad dog that we face.

And the effects of runaway stress responses aren't limited to anxiety and tension. Because flight-or-fight responses increase heart rate and constrict blood vessels, more blood gets pumped into smaller spaces, causing blood pressure to rise. In addition to hypertension, mismanaged stress also contributes to ailments such as heart illness and diminished immune system functioning.

Men and women tend to experience different situations as stressful—and they have different physical reactions to stress. In a recent study by investigators at Ohio State University's Institute for Behavioral Medicine Research, 90 newly wed couples were observed engaging in conflict. While they argued, their physical stress responses were measured. During the conflict, women's blood pressure rose most. Women also experienced a dramatic surge in the stress hormones cortisol and norepinephrine. By the next day, the women's white blood cell counts were down, indicating that their immune functioning had deteriorated. The majority of men, on the other hand, remained physically unaffected by the altercation.

These researchers duplicated their findings with couples married an average of 42 years. In both studies, the pursuer-distances dance described earlier had particularly damaging long-term consequences for women. When men respond to conflict by withdrawal, avoidance, or denial and women correspondingly escalate their demands and accusations, the women's health may be damaged. The good news? When couples in the two studies resolved conflicts constructively, the women did not suffer ill effects.

"I'm Too Tired to Fight or Run Anymore."

Your body is remarkably self-protective. If you do not calm runaway fight-or-flight reactions, the next stage of the stress response serves as a stop-gap maneuver to keep you from burning out. Your body begins to shut down via the *conservation-withdrawal response.*

Conservation-withdrawal response is the physical opposite of fight-or-flight response: Blood pressure lowers and secretions of stress hormones lessen. In combination, these two responses take you from overdrive (fight-or-flight) to underdrive (conservation-withdrawal). Conservation-withdrawal response is probably the mechanism underlying the vital exhaustion syndrome described previously.

Going Numb: The Price Paid for Conservation-Withdrawal Response

Although this may at first seem like a welcome calming of a stress storm, it is a rather tricky reaction. While conservation-withdrawal response protects us from one form of stress, it leaves us vulnerable to others. This is because the initial calm grows into numbness that leads to physical, emotional, and relationship problems.

Simply put, numbness is dangerous. When people are numb, they lose their ability to know when to make adjustments necessary to interrupt the wear-and-tear effects of stress. The result? Our bodies, emotions, and relationships begin to show damage.

Pain is your body's helpful way of alerting you to danger. The numbness of the conservation-withdrawal response can complicate physical health in various ways.

- Autoimmune system responses are dampened, which may explain why so often we don't get sick until after a stress-filled time has passed.

- Uncontrolled stress reactions interfere with our ability to think clearly. Blunted concentration and attention leads to more accidents.

Similarly, if we become emotionally numb, we don't notice when we need to change activities so that our exhausted energy supplies can recuperate. We just plow on, losing our creativity and sense of joy in the process.

In this state of numb exhaustion, we lose abilities that are crucial to keeping our relationships alive. Here, people do not damage their relationships due to the typical stress reactions of hurriedness, anxiety, or irritability. Their only symptom is their lack of feelings—joy, energy, enthusiasm, satisfaction, humor, creativity, concentration, sex drive, and/or flexibility.

Most often, the numbness of conservation-withdrawal reactions comes from mismanagement of our personal stress reactions. But some people go numb because of their unhappiness about major aspects of their lives. They may be living in some toxic territory. They may be suffering unrelenting marital problems, or career problems, or living in physical surroundings they find alarming and irritating. They go numb to endure.

Regardless of its cause, numbness signals a true need for change. Otherwise you will enter the next stage of the stress response, exhaustion.

Running on Empty

Think of your ability to cope as dependent on the availability of a precious fuel, called *adaptation energy*. Pretend that you have only a limited amount of this coping energy available at any point in time, and that it is divided across a number of fuel tanks. Each of these tanks serves a specific purpose—giving you energy to cope with specific activities or stresses. Dealing with both positive (wanted, enjoyable) and negative (unwanted, unpleasant) aspects of your life requires that you burn adaptation energy.

Whenever you need to adapt, your body draws fuel from the appropriate energy tank. As long as you are actually dealing with that stress *or* vividly thinking about that stress, you are burning fuel from the corresponding adaptation energy tank. In this way, you might burn energy from multiple tanks at once. For example, you may be chatting with your children while thinking of problems at work. The result? You lose coping energy both from the dealing-with-family fuel tank and the coping-with-work-stress fuel tank.

If you draw energy from a given tank for too long, your body and your mind signal that it is time to switch tanks. The alarm that you are running out of available adaptation energy on a given tank may come in different forms.

- When you do anything beyond the point of comfort, your body gives you *physical* signals that it's time for a change. For example, after working at your computer for a while, your eyes might begin to feel strained, or your body might begin to ache from prolonged sitting.
- You might also experience *emotional* signals that it's time for a change. Perhaps you become restless or aggravated as you grow bored with what you are doing. The information on the computer screen seems to aggravate rather than stimulate you.
- Finally, your *cognitive* (thinking) functions might also begin to shut down: Your concentration slips; you begin to have difficulty thinking abstractly; your memory begins to fail you.

If you sensibly respond to these warning signals by switching to a less-stressful activity, no harm is done. But as a high-powered coper, you are probably expert at going numb and keeping on going. In stress terms, this means that you are a pro at not responding to the signals from your body, your emotions, and your mind, warning that you are running out of gas in a given coping tank. While this talent might serve you well in allowing you to work hard, doing so can seriously hurt your body, your emotions, your creativity, and most important, your relationship.

Noticing the signals that your body and your mind give you regarding your stress reactions is a crucial first step toward BEST.

Handling Change

Any change is stressful. Both positive and negative changes require you to adjust, and therefore both cause stress. We can't ignore that a recent job promotion, a new house or baby, or even a recent financial inheritance can be almost as stressful as it is soothing.

Change also comes in two flavors—continuous and discontinuous. We borrow here from the wisdom of consultant Ernie Lawson:

> If you place a frog in a pot of cold water, then put the pot on a stove, the frog will happily swim around. It won't notice the subtle changes in the water's rising temperature until it is too late, and the heated water kills it.
>
> If you place a frog into a pot of boiling water, however, the shock of the change will alarm the frog and it will jump out.

The first instance is an example of a *continuous change*. The increments in the change process are so small that they go unnoticed. Change of this sort gradually erodes intimacy in relationships, motivation in the workplace, or our physical health.

The second instance is an example of a *discontinuous change*, the sort that is accompanied by alarms and whistles signalling that something big is happening. This type of change occurs when a loved one has an affair, or colleagues lose their jobs, or your physical self-image is changed forever by an unwanted diagnosis. While this type of change slaps us into paying attention to what is happening, we can often look back and notice subtle signs that the change was coming.

If we cope by hunkering down, going numb, and keeping on going, we risk ignoring continuous changes until we collide with one form or another of discontinuous change. We fail to notice the connection between ourselves and our loved ones evaporating, the morale slipping away in our workplace, or the signs that our health is failing.

Does the Change Fit Your Style?

It is important to be honest about the fit between your coping style and the flavor of change you are facing. Some people shine during an acute crisis. But they might not do so well in managing a slowly progressing, meandering change process. They like closure, and changes that poke along stress them more than any crisis.

Other people prefer slowly moving change and are paralyzed by acute crises. These folks cope well with stresses such as a ponderous reorganization at work, but they are overloaded by crises that demand a quick response. For example, they might have difficulty coping with a loved one's unexpected hospitalization, even though they may cope well with a loved one's chronic illness. Or, they may experience stress overload in response to news that their families have to relocate quickly because of career changes, but they might cope well once the relocations are made.

How Do We Cope?

Change management expert Elizabeth Harper-Neeld noted the various ways that different members of a work team might react to change. Her observations also apply to the ways couples and families cope as they go from one stage of life to the next. For example, as we move from parenting children to parenting adolescents; or as our parents' aging increases our levels of concern and hands-on involvement in their lives; or as our relationships enter a new stage of romance, different people might react with:

- *Anxiety.* We become terrified by the implications of the change.
- *Denial.* We pretend that the change is temporary and will go away if we just wait long enough.
- *Illusions of control.* Our anxiety is momentarily soothed by over-focusing on some issue or task or goal. We believe that if we can just argue a single point loudly enough, or manage a single issue perfectly enough, or pursue a single goal relentlessly enough, then our anxiety about the larger changes we are facing will disappear.
- *High-powered coping.* We do what is needed, even if we don't welcome the change. We get on board with the new program, learn what we can about the new territory, and move on. The surprise here is the discovery that this new territory contains more and more changes. Just when we figure we have peaked on our performance and endurance curves, we are faced with yet another demand. This might take the form of another bout of acting out by our adolescent; another health problem in our aging parent; another crisis in our relationship; or yet another paradigm shift at work.

Keys for Managing the Stress of Change

1. *Remember: any change is stressful.* Even positive, exciting changes are stressful because they place you in unfamiliar territory.

Be sensitive to changes that loved ones are facing, even those that are positive.

2. *Exercise choice when choosing is possible.*   Don't jump at every opportunity that your Big Life presents. When possible, be selective and respectful of yourself and your loved ones in timing major changes. Pause before accepting an opportunity to change, even if the change is positive and exciting. Ask yourself whether the prices you will pay adjusting to the change make the stress worthwhile—for you and for your loved ones. Be sure to ask loved ones how they feel about any change that you are considering.

Evaluate your current life circumstance honestly, with an eye toward determing whether you *want* the change and whether there is room in your life for this change *at this time.* Be realistic and honest. It takes courage to clarify your values and live according to your convictions. Don't let offers that come from your circumstances or from others write the script that is *your* life.

3. *Choose how you will think about your decision.*   If you choose to decline making the change at this time, remember that if the change is important enough, there will be time during the course of life to make it happen. If it doesn't happen, then life has a way of rendering it unimportant.

If you voluntarily say no to an opportunity to change, it is important for you and your loved ones to come to conceptual harmony about this decision. This means clarifying how you will think about your decision—as a couple or a family. When possible, conceptualize such a decision as an indication of bravery, good judgement, wisdom, maturity, or love for each other. Take advantage of the moment: See the decision to pass on this opportunity to change as an opportunity to underscore your commitment to cooperating with each other to BEat Stress Together.

Finally, don't be afraid to take a leap of faith here and to encourage each other to do the same. Believe in your ability to recreate similar options in the future, if you so desire. Believe in your collective abilities to adjust to the loss of passing up what might seem like a golden opportunity. If you decide to pass on this opportunity, decide also to be relieved that you dodged the stress that would have come with the change.

4. *Believe.*   We cope best when we trust our course of action. Whether it is the reorganization taking place at work or your family's transition to a new stage of family life, you have to find a way to believe in the goodness of what is afloat. In some cases, this means making sense of your suffering.

5. *Don't add fuel to the fire.*   Once a change is afloat, don't make the mistake of attempting to cope by creating additional, unnecessary changes.

We seem particularly prone to commit this mistake when faced with unwanted changes. For example, people suffering the end of a romance or marriage often amplify their pain by adding unnecessary endings to the list of what is already stressing them. They may decide to end friendships or drop out of organizations that they used to enjoy as a couple. Some even decide to move and start a new life.

Wiping the slate clean and starting over can be an effective stress management strategy. However, first give yourself time to absorb the blow and the stress of the major change you are facing. Then, when the dust of your initial emotional reactions settles, look clearly at your options. Examine those parts of your life you want to change while adjusting to the change that you might not have wanted.

6. *Underscore what will not change.*   Fearing the unknown makes changing difficult. One way to soothe this fear is to take note of what will remain the same. Whether dealing with a new stage of family life or a new policy at work, specify, to the best of your ability, what life will be like once this change is implemented.

7. *Take extra care.*   Change is not only stressful, it can be scary. Stamina doesn't come from fear; it comes from being nurtured and

understood. It is important to remember to take extra care of yourself and your loved ones during times of major change.

Destressing Your Environment

We spend so much of our time in crowded, noisy spaces that increase our heart rates, tense our muscles, and significantly raise our aggravation levels that we often don't recognize our environment as a stress factor.

Do the look, sound, feel, and smell of your surroundings matter to you? Imagine that you are walking into your house or apartment after a stressful day. You open the door and are hit with the blast of a radio playing in one room and a television blaring in another room. The phone rings, and one of your family members begins a loud conversation, adding to the din.

As you enter your kitchen, you glance around and notice that, once again, it's a total mess. Newspapers are lying beside the breakfast table. The morning dishes are still in the sink. Articles of clothing are draped over the chairs. Last week's mail is piled high on the counter tops. The smell of dirty dishes and the overflowing trash fills your nostrils. Notice how you feel as you vividly imagine arriving home to such a mess.

Now change the scene. Take a deep breath. Relax. In your mind's eye, picture your house or apartment as it is after you have straightened and cleaned it. Starting with the area you first enter as you open the door, see each room. Everything is in its place. Your clean kitchen is invitingly neat. Dishes and clothes are put away. Trash has been picked up. Throughout your home, things are clean and inviting.

Now imagine walking into this clean, orderly house after a stressful day. This time you are met with the pleasant sounds of softly playing music and the fresh, inviting aroma of a bouquet of fresh flowers. Notice how you feel this time as you imagine entering your neat and tidy kitchen.

Keys for Managing Environmental Stress

1. *Don't add insult to injury.*   If you are already stressed, do what you can to destress your environment. Slow down. Remind yourself that rushing assaults your body and emotions. Turn off distracting sounds or visuals, especially when you are trying to communicate. Go to a room that offers less stimulation when you want to talk. Make time to keep your workspaces uncluttered so that stressful activities become less stressful.

2. *Do what you can to create a pleasant resting place, and visit it regularly.*   This does not mean that you have to regularly go on vacation to a beautiful resort to manage stress. Rather, you should make it a part of your daily or weekly routine to visit some favorite spot in your yard, your home, or your community. Even a favorite chair can be a private relaxation base.

Building a Life in Harmony with Your Values

Are you living out of harmony with your inner values? We get knocked out of position by filling our days with activities that do not align with our inner needs and values and cause tension. The Values Inventory chart on page 121 lists 20 words that describe aspects of life that are valued by different people to different degrees.

In evaluating your responses, consider that most of us have only 25 to 35 hours of free time available each week, once we subtract from our 168-hour week the amount of time we use sleeping, working, and attending to our various obligations. Most of us waste at

---

VALUES INVENTORY

Security	Acceptance
Status	Power
Being liked	Achievement
Recognition	Authority
Approval	Service to others
Affection	Glamour
Belongingness	Money
Meaningful friendships	Meaningful family relationships
Spirituality	Fun
Adventure	Physical health

1. Separately, not as a couple, rank the top five values as they apply to you. Be honest. Don't list what you know you *should* value or what your spouse or family values.
2. Reread the list, and this time rank the *bottom* five: Which are the aspects of life that are *least* important to you?

---

least half of this free time doing things that have nothing to do with what we value.

Ask yourself this question: During the last week, how much of your available time did you spend actively doing something that was in harmony with your top five values?

Finally, share your respective lists of values. Notice how you are similar or different, where you agree or disagree. Discuss the importance of the values you have checked. Especially note values that you may hold dear but fail to act on often enough. Why is this? Do the demands of your life (such as having to travel for business) thwart your ability to act on other values (such as being present for your family)?

Managing the Stress of Being Out of Synch with Your Values

1. *Support each other.*   Remind yourself and each other of the values that you believe in. Remember that stress-hardy people make it a priority to behave in harmony with their values *as much as is realistically possible.* When living aligned with our values is not possible, support and understanding from loved ones is crucial. See what you are facing—even the stressful parts of your life together—as having meaning in terms of your values. Express appreciation to each other for being allies in the journey.

2. *At first, think small.*   Identify what you can do—even in a small way—to increase the alignment between the ways you choose to spend your life and your inner yearnings or needs. Regularly pause to ask yourself: "What do I (or we) really think, feel, need, or want right now?" Honestly answering this question may lead to surprising insights about two things: (1) How often you sell yourselves out by *not* behaving in harmony with your inner selves, and (2) how many small opportunities present themselves in the course of a typical day to create better alignment with your values.

3. *Believe in yourself.*   The road to inner peace and a smoother ride through the stress of your life is paved with small choices that align your behavior with your inner values. Finding the courage to believe in and experiment with small (or large) changes in this realm is a key to BEST.

Resolving Role Conflicts

Work, family, intimate relationships, self. No one lives in perfect balance across these arenas. Factors such as age, stage of family life, career development, or individual interests and passions cause us to periodically focus more on one area than another. This does not necessarily lead to problems unless we consistently overfocus on a given area and ignore others. The best bet is striving to manage periods of imbalance most effectively.

Managing the Stress of Multiple Roles

1. *Call it what it is.* Begin by asking yourself what the momentum of your life is compelling you to overfocus on: work, family, intimate relationships, or yourself. Remember, this momentum might be fueled by any combination of factors: your stage of life; your current life circumstance; your excitement, enthusiasm, and passion about some aspect of your life; or your overall pattern of stressors. Answer the same question regarding your most intimate partner.

2. *Go for good enough.* The goal here is *reasonable balance across arenas over long periods of time.* Perfect balance is neither possible nor necessary. But you should beware of long-term, extreme neglect of one or more areas. Even during stages of life that preoccupy you with the demands coming from one arena, it is important to at least periodically make it a priority to attend to the neglected arenas.

3. *Ask your partner for feedback.* It is sometimes difficult to accurately observe yourself. Feedback from our partners can clarify what and how we need to change to live in more healthy balance. If you pair your request for input with a sincerely expressed desire to do what you can to improve your overall teamwork, you are much more likely to receive helpful, caring feedback.

Finding (or Making) Time

In many ways, time seems to be the culprit in managing stress. It often seems to be the enemy that pushes us to try harder, move faster, and feel bad because we never complete all the work of our life before it runs out. It is crucial to regularly create time to nurture yourself. Put aside your work and your worries and do something that brings you pleasure and rejuvenation. Doing so will increase your energies and improve your performance in other important areas of your life.

There are two types of high-powered copers. First are the true exceptions to the notion that living under high levels of stress is harmful. These people thrive in both their professional and personal lives, even as they juggle enormous amounts of objectively measured stress.

On the other hand, these are people who in many ways resemble the exceptional copers described above: they are high-powered, super-competent people living the Big Life and struggling to survive its wear and tear. But the operative word here is *struggle*. Unlike their thriving colleagues, these folks show telltale signs of stress and burnout.

What differentiates these two versions of high-powered performers is how they manage time. The first group takes time to diversify. They fill their weeks with different activities that allow their main adaptation energy tanks regular breaks. The result? By diversifying, they constantly draw fresh adaptation energy from relatively full tanks. No wonder they perform so well!

What these healthy high-powered copers do *not* do frames our recommendations for managing the stressor of time.

Keys to Managing the Stress of Time

1. *Don't wait until.* The strugglers of the world make several mistakes that complicate rather than help their attempts to manage themselves. First, these are people who hunker down, intent on enduring a narrowly focused lifestyle (and on delaying their enjoy-

ment of their lives) until some goal is attained or some stressor goes away. This might mean waiting until the kids grow up and move out before they start enjoying their romances. Or waiting until they get promotions before joining their families. Or waiting until they attain some ideal body image before starting to enjoy themselves and their partners sexually.

Of course, it's not necessarily a mistake to intensely focus your energies while pursuing meaningful goals. In fact, such focused quests usually begin with a great deal of commitment, challenge, and control—the necessary ingredients for healthy stress.

But what started out as an *event* that would have a clear beginning, middle, and end often becomes a *process* that lasts a lifetime. *Waiting until* can then translate into waiting for the rest of your life.

Second, most folks narrowly focus their energies as they devote themselves to the quest or the major stress at hand. They gradually withdraw from others, drift into less and less playfulness, and may even lose sight of what they find pleasurable. In short, they stop diversifying and burn out.

2. *Don't settle for variations of the theme.* Some people adopt stress management strategies that they think are diversifications, but that in reality are simply variations of the theme that is draining them. Consider David:

> David worked as a vice president of finance in a major corporation. He was referred by his company's Director of Health Promotions due to the company's dissatisfaction with his temper outbursts and his generally ineffective management style. He had also recently made major errors during a highly visible corporate strategic planning session. His company valued his history of loyalty and devotion, but his recent problems had raised serious questions regarding his overall competence as a senior executive. The combination of concern for David and uncertainty regarding his future with the company led to his referral.

It quickly became clear that David was burned out from his relentless job involvement. He had been promoted to vice president four years prior and responded to this achievement with the commitment to prove himself capable and competent at this high level of corporate visibility. David explained: "My wife and I talked about this for weeks before we decided that I would accept the challenge of showing the world that I can run with the big dogs. We agreed that if I proved myself during my first five years as vice president, then we'd probably be set for life. This is my big chance. It's what I have always wanted. My wife and I agreed on this; she has committed herself to helping me do this, even if it means making temporary sacrifices in our personal lives."

As you read further excerpts from our conversations with David, notice how he is living out his confusion about what is and what is not true diversification of activities. Unfortunately, what David considers breaks from work are actually no more than variations on the theme of work. His attempts at creating self-nurturing solutions to job stress are simply variations on job involvement, not breaks from the constant drain on his job-related adaptation energy channel.

I don't understand how you could think that I might not be managing the stress of my work. I hate crunching numbers. What I really enjoy is managing people. So, when I get stressed I kick back for an hour or so and read books on management. This helps prepare me in other areas important to my work.

I also only schedule lunchtime business meetings with people that I like. After all, I don't want to live with constant indigestion.

During my commuting time, I like to listen to audiotapes on management and motivation. This always gives me food for thought about how to deal with my people.

I never let my at-home paperwork interfere with sitting down and eating dinner with my family. I wait and do my paperwork after dinner, when the kids are preoccupied with their homework.

I like to end the day by reading a little in bed—usually something light, like a psychology book or a nontechnical trade journal. You know, stuff that is good to know, but not too painful to learn.

David is living in his version of a prevalent, subtle trap that is difficult for him to avoid because many of his choices do make solid stress management sense. For example, it is wise to sandwich undesirable work tasks between those that are more desirable. It's also wise to further educate yourself in areas that fuel a sense of control and interest in important aspects of your career.

However, these work management strategies are not the same as our BEST strategy of diversifying your activities. David's strategies all drain energy from one place—the channel that contains work-related adaptation energy. Each of these activities is a variation on the same theme—work. Admittedly, some of the work tasks are more desirable and enjoyable for David than others, but the fact remains that this man spends virtually every waking hour working. No wonder he is burning out.

BEating Stress Together involves many things: helping each other through change, collaboratively destressing your environment, doing a value check, resolving role conflicts, and finding time. We've found that for most people, the last component is the toughest. That's because many of us suffer from hurry sickness.

Chapter Nine

Slowing Down on the Fast Track

As we approach the 21st century, success in the workplace requires the same skills that successful personal relationships require: negotiating, team building, nurturing, and conflict avoidance. High-powered people have a dilemma both at home and at work: They need to get along with the same people they are colliding with as they race through their days. This perpetual treadmill is called *hurry sickness,* and it's no wonder so many of us suffer from it.

We constantly hear, and often internalize, messages from the management gurus: "Make yourself indispensable." "Stay hands-on involved in all aspects of your team's operations." "If you aren't gaining, you are losing."

Despite the consultants' advice, in increasing numbers we are choosing to slow down and shift gears. So, if you or your partner refuse to stay lost in someone else's work-addicted values, you are not alone.

Surveys in the 1990s have found that only approximately 30 percent of respondents saw work as the most important thing in their lives—a record low. A 1996 survey released by Robert Half International Inc., revealed that nearly two-thirds of Americans would reduce their hours and compensation in exchange for more "family or personal time."

We have known many couples who found the courage to shrink their Big Life. But when it comes to managing their combined roles, they remain overworked. Maybe you don't spend 60 to 90 hours each week in the office. But do you spend much time playing, relaxing, contemplating, planting flowers, or meandering with your loved ones? Such life-balancing experiences won't happen unless you develop a realistic plan to counter hurry sickness.

Going for Good Enough

High-powered people who manage to become Dynamic Duos do not stop working. Rather, they change their pace and activities. If they work or commute together, they are mindful to not hurt each other with hurriedness. If they do not see each other during the work-day, self-management helps them save coping energy that enhances their time together in the evenings. The following 20 strategies can help you slow down the pace of your life and give you and your relationships a chance to thrive and not simply struggle to survive.

1. *Start slowly.* Begin your day with a few minutes of silence. Meditate or simply picture your day unfolding with reasonable smoothness. Include in this meditation images of your remaining open, calm, and focused when interacting with loved ones.

2. *Pay attention to your comfort zone.* Quietly pay attention to your breathing and to the most relaxed part of your body while your car is warming up or as you settle into your commute. If you commute with your partner, use at least half the time to get out of your thoughts and pay attention to each other.

3. *Stay aware.*   Throughout your initial trip from home, repeat-edly notice and then release signs of tension. Loosen your hands if they are wrapped tightly around the steering wheel. Relax your shoulders if they are raised. Remember, being tense does not help you drive better or make your commute go faster.

4. *Be still.*   Learn to be comfortable being alone without distract-ing your attention from your inner self. Take time during your commute to turn off the radio or tape player. Soon enough, your day will begin to swirl with activities that take you out of self-awareness.

5. *Slow down.*   Purposely slow your pace, even if doing so requires that you leave home 10 minutes earlier. Drive at or below the speed limit. Remember, it is easier to control yourself if you stay in control of your pace. Practice courtesy to others.

6. *Get out of your head and into your senses.*   Pay attention to your breathing, to the colors around you, to the feel of your body on the seat. Fill your head with benign, sensory information, so that there is no room for anxiety-provoking thoughts or images.

7. *Get your bearings before you begin.*   Upon arriving at work but before you enter your office, take a few moments in the parking lot or while waiting for the elevator to orient yourself to your workday and to pinpoint three things that you are looking for-ward to doing or someone you are looking forward to interact-ing with at work.

8. *Relax before you start.*   While seated at your desk or work sta-tion but before beginning work, take a moment to scan your body for signs of tension and relaxation. Consciously attempt to relax and let go of excess tension.

9. *Brake to break the tension.*   Stop working for a minute or two every hour and truly relax rather than simply pause. Avoid cof-fee or cigarettes. Instead, take brief walks (even two minutes

helps). Or, sit at your work station, close your eyes, and recall a pleasant fantasy. When possible, use these breaks to touch base with loved ones, even if only by phone. These are not times to discuss problems with your partner. Agree that when you speak with each other during the day, you will try to be a source of encouragement and a reminder of the loving support that you have for each other.

10. *Change your environment.*   At least once during the day, get completely away from your work. Eat lunch away from your desk or office. If you and your partner meet for lunch, agree ahead of time whether this will be a working lunch—one during which you will discuss the issues and stresses of your life—or a support lunch. If you dine alone, choose to eat in silence once or twice each week. Eat slowly, and simply be with yourself. Don't work. Don't read. Just eat, and be still.

11. *Never start without first stopping.*   Before restarting work after lunch, take a few moments to consciously relax.

12. *Cue yourself.*   Use everyday cues in your environment as reminders to recenter yourself. For example, allow the phone to ring several times before answering; use those moments to pause, not rush. Program yourself to associate hanging up the phone, waiting for the elevator, opening a desk drawer, or changing a file on your computer screen with the reminder: "Relax, center, clear my mind, do one thing at a time."

13. *Take people breaks.*   Take some time during each day to share some nonwork-related information with your coworkers. Make an effort to show interest in important details in the other person's personal life.

14. *Show your human side.*   Each week, disclose a worry or regret to a trusted associate. Showing others your vulnerabilities keeps you in touch with yourself and helps thaw out your own numbness.

15. *Make a got-it-done list.*   End your workday by retracing your activities, acknowledging and congratulating yourself for what you have accomplished. Don't just list what you did *not* get done today (the proverbial to-do list for tomorrow); also note what you *did* get done today, and feel good about it.

16. *Accept; don't struggle.*   As you return to your car or ride home, pay attention to your breathing, the smells and sounds around you, the feeling of cold or warmth of your body, perhaps your own fatigue. Accept these sensations; don't resist them. Walk without feeling rushed.

17. *Prepare to be home.*   While commuting home, consciously prepare for the transition from work to home. Notice yourself slowing your pace. Stop rushing. Picture the people you will see when you arrive home and what you will do to connect with and enjoy them. Note at least two things you will do this evening to nurture yourself in a healthy way. If you commute with your spouse, allow time to destress from the workday before forcing communication with each other.

18. *Remember whom you are dealing with.*   As you arrive home, take a minute to orient yourself to being with your loved ones. Remember: No superpeople live here. Switch gears to be with the people who matter most to you.

19. *Say hello.*   It has probably been a long day of absence from each other. Changing out of your work clothes will be a welcome relief and help you transit into your next role. But first say hello to each of your family members. Take just a few minutes to connect with each of them. Ask how they are doing, how their days went, and pay attention to their answers. Then excuse yourself, take a few minutes to be quiet and still, switch roles (and clothes), and join your family.

20. *Remember that you deserve a recess.*   Resist the temptation to fill your at-home time with endless homework. Remind each other

that, indeed, even the hardest working people deserve a recess. Taking time today to enjoy your home and your family is the best way to rejuvenate yourself in preparation for tomorrow.

Four Keys to Treating Hurry Sickness

The strategies listed are effective ways to disrupt hurry sickness. Practice makes them second nature and naturally creates a slower pace as the weeks unfold.

But hurry sickness won't improve until you dare to set limits and remain mindful of your choices on a level broader than your hour-to-hour lifestyle. It is crucial to learn to create boundaries that separate you alone, and as a couple, from the demands of the world around you. By learning to periodically say no to your inner drivenness and to the demands of your Big Life, you create the circumstances that give you and your relationships a chance to stay healthy.

Saying No Takes Several Forms

1. *Schedule unplanned days.* Set aside at least one day each month that is proclaimed an unplanned day. Meander through it together, even though you might at first feel anxious.
2. *Think small.* The best acts of self-nurturing come in small doses. In addition to attending to your responsibilities and compulsions, dare to take time for pleasure, not productivity. Take a nap. Read something for its entertainment value. Watch a movie, or take a walk together that is *not* according to your exercise schedule. Remember, there are 336 half-hour stretches of time in each of your weeks. You can afford to simply enjoy some of them—alone and together—and many more will remain for completing your work.

3. *Trust yourself.*   Many high-powered people are frightened of their ability to rebel. They fear that if they start relaxing, playing, time-shifting, or otherwise thawing out from their numbness, they'll completely drop out. But taking time out can lead to more healthy, satisfying relationships and keep us happy and motivated at work.

4. *Use a join-your-family beeper.*   This recommendation comes from writers David Waters & J. Terry Saunders, who make the poignant point that we regularly let the beepers of our age disconnect us from each other. Whether from phone calls, faxes, pagers, express mail, or the simple requests of others, we turn over control of our time to external sources. Consider: "What would happen if you had a beeper that regularly sounded the alarm to 'Join your family?'"

For those of you who live and die by your computers' calendars or time management journals, why not use those same tools to remind yourselves to call home, send flowers, take a night off, ask about that school project, or other cues to connect you with your loved ones.

A Word of Caution

Two surprises greet you when you reestablish contact between your mind and body after years of numbness. First comes the anxiety that signals your entry into new territory. No matter how healthy that territory might be, it is still unfamiliar. Remember that bearing through this anxiety is a price that must be paid for positive change.

Next come anger and sadness. As we will discuss in Chapter Eleven, anger often masks sadness over losses. As you thaw out and begin to enjoy a less traumatizing pace of life, you will notice that you, too, enjoy the basics, such as relaxing, connecting with others, resting when you are tired, or giving yourself well-deserved rewards. Juxtaposed with this pleasure, you might notice anger and sadness over the many times you denied yourself these basics.

Most people in recovery progress from wariness to aggravation with those who don't embrace their newly found philosophies. As you change, it is important to manage your reactions to others, especially your loved ones who may not yet be embracing your change with a fervor that matches your own.

Respect Each Other's Pace

Not everyone changes on the same schedule. This fact can frustrate you and those around you. Health psychologist James Prochaska and his colleagues have noted that we tend to progress through predictable stages in changing any health behavior. We have noted that a similar progression occurs when we try to create better balance in our lives.

In *precontemplation*, we have no intention of changing and find ways to rationalize our continuing in old ways. We ignore pleas or advice from loved ones that slowing down and creating a better balance is necessary.

During *contemplation* we begin to notice and think about our need to change, but we are not yet ready to actually do anything differently. We may decide to read books (such as this one), talk about the need to slow down, and listen to loved ones' laments about the same. But we are not yet ready to commit to changing.

Preparation begins when we voice our intention to take action in the next few months. We begin experimenting with very small changes that create more balance. Here, we need encouragement and support—not preaching or nagging—from our partners.

Next comes *action*, when we begin making definite changes that lead to better balance. This is an awkward time for hard-driving people. We aren't accustomed to balance; we're used to working. Particularly during the first six months of changing, we need participation, cooperation, and applause from loved ones— reminders that learning to feel comfortable with a reasonable pace and style of life is the right fight to fight.

After six months of living with our changes, we enter *maintenance*. The work now is to prevent relapses into old ways and avoid over-reacting to slips into overworking. We can help each other maintain reasonable balance by verbalizing pride and appreciation in each others' efforts, and by encouraging—rather than doubting or lamenting "I knew this wouldn't last"—when a backslide happens.

What if work and family pressures are beyond your control? We know that many people live and work in settings that require huge personal sacrifices. Two-fifths of today's workers say that work has a negative impact on their home lives, and the policies that so profoundly effect their lives are often not under their control. As of 1995, 73 percent of large companies claimed to have various work-family policies, but debate exists as to whether existing policies are making any positive difference for today's superachievers.

We struggle on whatever roads we choose to travel, and we grieve over the roads we choose not to travel. Nowhere is this more apparent than in our reactions as we notice each other's work-family balancing choices.

How do you react to men who limit their time at work? If you are like most, you probably wrestle with one of the two attitudes expressed by Ron, a corporate vice president for a large furniture manufacturer.

> I get to work every day before 7:00 a.m., and I never get home until after dark. That adds up to a bunch of 10- and 12-hour days. And the

work just keeps piling up. Yet I see these guys—my boss included—bolting every day at 5:00 or 5:30, come hell or high water. My boss even said to me that he thinks that I work too hard.

Maybe I do work too hard, but I think two things when I see him sticking to his eight-to-five commitment: (1) If he bit the bullet, we would more likely make those numbers that corporate is always hollering about; and (2) if he's going to be this slack, it's just a matter of time before I'll take his job.

Women, too, can be hurtful in their reactions to each other. This struggle is reflected in the comments of two of our clients, Sharon and Joyce. These women worked together in a thriving accounting firm. Neither knew that the other was consulting us.

Sharon: The most painful part of my pregnancy leave was my friend Joyce's attitude. She kept making snide comments like, "Who do you think is taking up your slack while you're out nursing that new baby?" She was worse than any of the men in our office. Just because she never had kids, she seems to expect every woman in the office to be as career-oriented as she is.

I don't know what she's complaining about. Half the time I wish I was her. I see her and her husband making loads of money, traveling all over the world, and basically enjoying themselves. I go home every day and change diapers, carpool, and bear through another weekend of laundry.

Joyce: I love what I do; I love my husband. But I am ready for this family thing to go away. I keep struggling with whether we made the right decision, not having kids. I know that I have not resolved this issue: When women in our office go out on maternity leave, I resent them. It's not just the work problems they create by being out; it's the fact that their pregnancy rubs my life in my face. I've got to find a way to accept what I have chosen to do.

Finding the right balance between work and family is an individual issue. There are no right answers here. Both men and women report highest levels of happiness when they have both work and a bustling family life—not in balance, but in a reasonably controlled shuffle. As journalist Joseph Nocera reminded us, the "balance at all costs" mentality too often villainizes working hard. It's sometimes only honest to say to our families, "I love you guys, but I love my job too." It is a mistake to judge ourselves or others because their work-family choices differ from our own.

Staying stress resistant is especially difficult when you're struggling with hurry sickness, both at work and at home. Unless we slow our pace and stop to consider our loved ones' needs, our relationships will suffer. The ultimate determinant of our stress resistance is how well we manage ourselves and our relationships. For most of us, one necessary aspect of BEST is taking control of our situations, processes, and relationships.

Chapter Ten

Overcoming Supercouple
Syndrome

We have discussed what stress is. We have encouraged you to begin looking at your specific stress symptoms—your physical, behavioral, emotional, and relationship red flags that signal when a stress swirl is in motion. We hope we have also stirred your thinking about the typical causes of your stress and ways you can counter hurry sickness and its effects in your relationships.

We turn now to designing a change program specific to your goals and needs. This starts with learning how your fantasies can show you the way.

Psychological and behavioral habits die hard. Some people actually believe that such changes are not possible. They justify staying in their overlearned ways of coping (or moping) with attitudes like: "You can't teach an old dog new tricks"; "I am who I am, and no one has the right to ask me to change"; "Being this way just runs in our family"; "After so many years of being together, what can you expect? This is just the way it's going to be."

We spend our careers challenging beliefs like these. We have seen thousands of people change themselves and their relationships. Along the way, we have noticed that regardless of the specifics of the situation, certain universals apply when it comes to changing. We have systematized our observations into a simple model for creating a change contract. Start by finding the wisdom in your fantasies.

Changing Fantasies into Action Plans

Most of us regularly long to do something different with our lives. This longing might start as relatively small stirrings of curiosity about a new hobby, or a new acquaintance, or the latest developments in some field of study. Or you might find yourself fantasizing about a very different way of living: You might wonder what it would be like to do away with much of the stuff that clutters your life, move to a quieter place, live at a slower pace, and start over—with or without your partner.

It is certainly wise not to get lost in unrealistic fantasies that might lead you to trade one version of stress for another. But your fantasies can be a source of wisdom; they may signal what you need to change to reignite your passions and preserve your stamina. Don't ignore the obvious.

> If you consistently ignore your inner stirrings, they magnify—growing larger and larger—until you feel either: (a) that you will only be satisfied by an exaggerated version of what you originally wanted only a little of; or (b) that what you want is so unattainable, trying to change is futile.

The trick to using your fantasies as guides is to notice their themes and then allow yourself to fulfill some of those fantasies. This almost always involves making changes that more closely align the ways you are living with your inner needs and wants. To make change happen you usually have to shift your situations, processes, and relationships so that they satisfy your needs for challenge, commitment, and control.

Five Steps in Changing Fantasies into Plans

Changing fantasies into plans takes only five steps:

Step 1:   Specify your fantasy in words.

Step 2:   Be realistic about the problems you will face if you act on the fantasy.

Step 3:   Note your stress-generating reactions to the problems you will face if you try to fulfill your fantasy. (Hint: This will almost always involve talking yourself into staying in some form of misery.)

Step 4:   Note the kernels of wisdom in your fantasy solution. Assume that underlying your fantasy are grains of truth about what you think, feel, need, or want more or less of.

Step 5:   Pinpoint specific, realistic, relatively small changes you could make in your life starting right now that might take you one step in the direction of satisfying your fantasy.

Here's an example of a client who put the five steps into action.

> Tony complained of being bored with his 18-year marriage to Jackie. We encouraged him to consider that boredom per se might be his problem; not boredom specific to his marriage. His responses to this notion were telling.
>
> Step 1: *Fantasy.* "I'm bored to death by my marriage, by our friends, and by our community. Maybe I ought to leave. Or maybe we ought to sell out, pack up, and move to the coast. A new life and a new set of people—that's what I need!"
>
> Step 2: *Problem with the fantasy solution.* "I don't want to ruin my family. I'm bored, but I do still love Jackie. I also don't really dislike all of my friends, and I do like living in this community. If I left here, I would miss many of these people and this place. Plus, I'm not willing to disrupt the lives of my wife and kids just to satisfy my selfish fantasy."

Step 3: *Stress-generating reaction.* "What's wrong with me? Most people would readily trade places with me. I ought to just stop complaining and enjoy my life as it is."

Step 4: *Kernel of wisdom in the fantasy.* "I like change. Getting to know new things, new people, and new places—that's what turns me on."

Step 5: *BEST solution.* "I just met a new colleague at work who seems interesting and different. I could invite him to play tennis, or maybe just invite him to go to lunch and not do anything that puts us in competition. Maybe we could invite him and his wife out for dinner. I could also take that art class that I keep talking myself out of taking—just for the hell of it. Even though it wouldn't change my life, at least next week would be different and more challenging."

The Eight Steps of Changing

Most of us would benefit from making small choices in response to our inner needs. Tony's willingness to experiment with this concept helped him rejuvenate his interests and prevented him from wrecking havoc in his marriage, which was not the source of his malaise. By taking more reasonable care of himself and by finding more reasonable ways to respond to his self-focused interests, he was able to keep his marriage in perspective.

Once you examine your fantasies and daydreams, you should have an idea about what your needs are. But how can you make change happen? A full-scale change program takes only eight steps.

STEP 1:   HONESTLY DECIDE WHAT YOU *NEED* TO CHANGE, WHAT YOU *WANT* TO CHANGE, AND WHAT YOU *ARE WILLING* TO CHANGE.

As in many journeys, the first step is perhaps the most difficult: You probably can rattle off a long list of changes that other people would like for you to make. But change made for the sake of others seldom lasts. This is an issue you must decide for yourself.

What are the things that you know might improve your health or your happiness if you were willing to change them? Identify what you are doing or experiencing that bothers you. This might be a behavior (smoking, overworking, compulsive eating, living in isolation from others) or an emotion (anger, loneliness, anxiety).

Create a change inventory to answer this question. Be honest and thorough. Don't worry about whether you are ready to take action. Simply write down the changes that would probably improve your health or your happiness, if you would or could change.

Read your responses. Have you been completely honest with yourself? Is there anything else that you might add—however big or small—that you know would improve your health or happiness? If so, add those items now. Are there changes that don't really belong, items that someone else would dictate about you? If so, erase them.

Next comes the hard part. You must declare your initial targets of change. Begin by choosing something that matters to you and that you are reasonably confident you can change in some small way. If easily implemented changes in areas that are important to you are not on your list, add them.

STEP 2: IDENTIFY AND DISRUPT THE STEPS (DOMINOES) IN THE PROCESSES THAT KEEP YOU STUCK.

A key to BEST is learning to disrupt overlearned coping strategies. These strategies consist of coping steps that are like dominoes lined up on edge in a continuous stack. Some of these steps (dominoes) might be bodily reactions to stress, some might be behaviors, some might be thoughts, and some might be interactions with others—all of which affect how you think and act in response to different situations. By changing any of your usual next steps, you will generate new outcomes for yourself and in your relationships. What coping steps can you change?

Avoid two pitfalls in completing this step. Resist the temptation to put the faces of other people on your stressors. It's important to notice what you do that contributes to the outcomes that you want to change. Notice your moment-to-moment and day-to-day reactions to your own thoughts, feelings, needs, and wants.

Don't make the mistake of ignoring your most basic needs for the sake of focusing on big dissatisfactions. By giving up control of the small stuff, we end up depleted and frustrated, and we conclude that we will feel better only if we change some major, complex part of our lives.

Maybe you do need to make some major change. But more often you will start to feel and function significantly better if you simply take better control of your basic needs, the stuff that gets overlooked in the numbness that comes with high-powered living.

To find out if you are ignoring the small stuff, keep a journal for two weeks. Write down your needs and your behaviors in reacting to those needs.

The exercise on page 147 is designed to help you begin to identify whether your ways of coping are more stressful than soothing. In completing this exercise, notice physical, behavioral, emotional, and interpersonal red flags that indicate stress build-up. (You might find it helpful to first consult the example that follows this exercise.)

STEP 3:   SPECIFY HOW YOU WOULD LIKE TO BEHAVE OR FEEL AND IDENTIFY THE KIND OF PERSON YOU WISH YOU COULD BECOME.

What would you like to do instead of staying stuck? Focus on specific areas of change: How you manage your body; how you relate to your family; or how you react to your inner stirrings. It might also be helpful to remember when your life was healthier and happier.

IDENTIFYING COPING SEQUENCES
THAT BACKFIRE

Instructions: Choose one or more of the problems identified in your change inventory. Recall or imagine the typical sequence of thoughts, behaviors, and events over a two-to-three-week period that either create or complicate the problem.

Complete the following sentences.

I tend to experience _____ (specify a problem reaction that you want to change) in the following way:

1. I feel _____.
2. I tell myself _____.
3. I then _____ (List an unhelpful attempted solution to 1 above).
4. The result of steps 1 to 3 tends to be that I _____ (List thoughts, feelings, and/or behaviors).
5. Next, I usually _____ (List a behavior, especially one directed at others).
6. Then, _____ (List someone in your life) begins _____ (List something that someone does to you).
7. I react by _____ (List something that you do in reaction to 6 above).
8. Then, I start telling myself _____.
9. I react to that sort of thinking by behaving like this: _____; and feeling like this: _____.
10. After being stuck in this struggle for a while, I _____ (List some self-defeating behavior or thought pattern).
11. I stay stuck by _____.

SAMPLE RESPONSES

I tend to experience *boredom, depression, and burnout* in the following way:

1. I feel *stuck in a rut.*
2. I tell myself *"there's nothing I can do about any of this."*
3. I then *preoccupy myself with fantasies that seem unreachable.*
4. The result of steps 1 to 3 tends to be that I *get sad and irritated.*
5. Next, I usually *withdraw into silence and get moody.*
6. Then, *my wife* begins to *question me, asking what is wrong. She also makes suggestions that she thinks might help.*
7. I react by *giving her abrupt, irritable responses.*
8. Then I start telling myself that *her questioning and nagging are my main problems.*
9. I react to that sort of thinking by behaving like this: *I vege out week after week, eat junk food, drink too much alcohol, and withdraw from my wife;* and feeling like this: *guilty that I'm such a slob and I panic—like I can't stand this life I'm living.*
10. After being stuck in this struggle for a while, I *start to fuss at myself about how fat and depressed I feel.*
11. I stay stuck by *talking myself out of doing anything different in any area of my life.*

If you can't recall a time when you were healthy and happy, you have two other options for completing Step 3. Notice the way someone you admire behaves and adopt goals for yourself based on those observations. Or, take guidelines from your own fantasies about the type of person you would like to be in the area that you have targeted to change.

While this can seem awkward, a key to BEST is finding the courage to change. Daring to specify how you would like to live in comparison to how you are living is an essential step in this process.

Do I Dare?

Remember the overused coping pattern that you identified in Step 2. Then, relax and fantasize that it is one year from now. Imagine that you run across this book while browsing through your bookshelf. As you thumb through its pages, imagine saying to yourself: "Compared to last year when I first read this book, I have really changed in a number of important ways. I am finally becoming more like the person I always wanted to be. These days, I am a person who _____."

Write down your fantasy of how you would like to be, instead of how you described yourself in Step 2.

STEP 4: IDENTIFY ONE OR TWO SPECIFIC CHANGES THAT WILL TAKE YOU ONE STEP IN THE DIRECTION OF THE FANTASY SPECIFIED IN STEP 3.

Focus on specific steps that are measurable, relatively easy to change, and that you are willing to begin changing immediately. Remember that this is a contract that you are making with yourself. Be honest. Commit to some realistic change that boils down to a single step toward your overall goal.

Start with a specific short-term goal that can realistically be reached in no more than two weeks. Your long-term goals are implied in your responses to Step 3. Here, you should focus on the only thing under your immediate control—your here-and-now choices. What are you willing to do starting right now that will take you one step in the direction of changing from the problems you identified in Steps 1 and 2 to the ways of living you identified in Step 3.

In your journal make two columns labeled *Instead of* and *I will*. In the first column list actions or behaviors you will avoid. In the second column list the things you will do instead to take you a step closer toward changing the problem you identified in Step 1. (Refer to Step 2 for a reminder of the self-defeating ways you typically react to this problem.) We've included a sample of this list on page 151 to help you in creating your own.

STEP 5: (1) LET SELECTED FAMILY OR FRIENDS KNOW WHAT YOU ARE DOING; (2) ASK FOR THEIR SUPPORT; AND (3) TELL THEM HOW THEY MIGHT BE SUPPORTIVE OF YOU.

High-powered people often make the mistake of believing that help and support from others is unnecessary. This flies in the face of a basic fact: We are social creatures. No matter how strong we are as individuals, others do affect us. None of us are islands. We need and profit from helpful input and support from others.

It's not only a mistake to think that you can change in any major way on your own; it's also a mistake to assume that other people innately know how to support you. You must teach the people in your life what you need from them to help you to change.

Our client, Tony, took the risk of explaining his struggles to his wife and was amazed at his own reactions.

> You know, in my professional life I'm known as The Hammer. When the deal needs to be made, I make it happen; I hammer the deal closed. Ask anyone who knows me, and they'll describe me as powerful and independent; and I am!
>
> What's interesting to me is how good it feels when Jackie gives me permission to take care of myself. As I'm leaving for a business trip, it means a lot when she reminds me to find time to relax on this trip and to take care of myself.
>
> If I'm so powerful, why am I so shy about giving myself this sort of permission? I don't know the answer. But one thing is for sure: You were right when you advised me to take a chance on letting my wife know that her encouragement helps me stick to this program. When Jackie is supportive it helps me feel more comfortable about taking

SAMPLE RESPONSE	
Instead of:	*I will:*
Remaining bored	Begin reading a new novel and attend the lecture on the Civil War that is being offered next Friday night.
Continuing to feel guilty about gaining weight	Begin a reasonable exercise plan that will involve taking at least two 45-minute walks, playing tennis once each week, and 15 minutes of calisthenics two times each week.
Staying socially stagnant	Invite my new business associate to lunch, and Jackie and I will invite my associate and his wife out to dinner.
Withdrawing from my wife	Initiate a conversation with my wife at least twice each day; invite her out to lunch two times each week; ask her questions about how she is doing, rather than leaving it up to her to carry our conversations.

better care of myself. Her support gives me a push to go ahead and do the right thing.

As you embark on any change program, you'll need to line up support from those closest to you. Use your journal to create a list of people you'll need to call on for support as you take steps toward changing the problems you identified. Next to the person's name list the specific things you'll ask them to do or understand to support you.

STEP 6:   REWARD YOURSELF EVERY DAY. SELF-NURTURING IS THE KEY TO MOTIVATING YOURSELF TO BEAR THROUGH THE DISCOMFORT OF CHANGING.

If change is to last, it must be rewarded. This sometimes happens automatically. For example: Improving your relationship leads to increased intimacy; or getting into better physical condition leads to enhanced self-confidence. But these major pay-offs may take awhile to blossom. In the meantime, it's important to structure in immediate rewards.

These might be simple: For example, give yourself permission to read something for pleasure or watch a favorite TV show that you might not typically take the time to watch. Take an extra-long, hot bath. Treat yourself to a favorite meal or visit someone you like. Take a few extra minutes to sit and enjoy the sights, sounds, and smells of nature before going about your day's work. Be nice to yourself. This is the key to feeling better and to making changes that last.

In your journal, write down four or five rewards that you will give yourself each day that you accomplish the things you have committed to doing to bring about change.

STEP 7:   DEVELOP A YARDSTICK THAT YOU CAN FREQUENTLY USE TO GIVE YOURSELF SPECIFIC FEEDBACK.

It is helpful to specify from the outset of your change program the questions that can be used to measure your progress. Every two weeks, use this yardstick to honestly evaluate how you are doing.

Be patient and realistic as you complete this step. Remember to be humble regarding your limitations. No one is perfect. At best our efforts are good enough to manage our ever-changing lives. Accepting this fact is not the same as settling for second best or denying that problems exist. Simply understand that striving for perfection will only make you and everyone around you miserable.

In your journal, write down the following statement:

> Two weeks from now, on the (Date _____ Month _____), I will evaluate my progress by noting whether I have changed in the following specific ways. (Refer back to the I will column from your Instead of/I will journal entry in completing this exercise.)

STEP 8:   RECONTRACT WITH YOURSELF AND YOUR LOVED ONES EVERY TWO WEEKS.

After evaluating your progress for two weeks, recontract your change program by repeating a version of Step 1. What have you learned from the past two weeks that can be applied to fine tune your change program? Do you feel frustrated because you asked too much of yourself? Are you having difficulty sticking to your program? Because you asked too little of yourself, do you need to stretch your goals for further motivation?

In your journal, note what you now want to change, but this time be sure to note what you are already doing that pleases you and that you want to continue. Compliment yourself for the progress that you are making. Remember: Go for good enough.

Putting It All Together

The principles and steps just described can help guide you to change in any way. Organize your responses to these exercises into a change contract.

A sample *change contract* is on pages 154 through 157, followed by a blank contract. Copy the blank contract before writing on it, so that you can periodically repeat this process.

SAMPLE CHANGE CONTRACT

With commitments to: (1) Be honest with myself; (2) stay aware; (3) find the courage to change; and (4) be humble enough to go for good enough, I *Tony* commit to the following contract.

Step 1:   I want to change the following about the way I am living or feeling: (1) *My boredom;* (2) *my repetitive social life;* (3) *blaming my wife for my problems.*

Step 2:   To do so, I need to remember that the feelings or behaviors specified in Step 1 occur as part of the following sequences:

1. I feel *stuck in a rut.*
2. I tell myself *there's nothing I can do about any of this.*
3. I then *preoccupy myself with fantasies that seem unreachable.*
4. The result of steps 1 to 3 is my *getting sad and irritated.*
5. Next, I usually *withdraw into silence and get moody.*
6. Then, *my wife* begins *to question me, asking what is wrong. She also makes suggestions that she thinks might help.*
7. I react by *giving her abrupt, irritable responses.*
8. Then I start telling myself that *her questioning and nagging are my main problems.*
9. I react to that sort of thinking by behaving like this: *I vege out week after week, eat junk food, drink too much alcohol, and withdraw from my wife;* and feeling like this: *guilty that I'm such a slob and panicked because I can't stand this life I'm living.*
10. After being stuck in this struggle for a while I *start to fuss at myself about how fat and depressed I feel.*
11. I stay stuck by *talking myself out of doing anything different in any area of my life.*

continued

Step 3:   Instead of continuing the pattern specified in Step 2, I would like to be the kind of person who:

1. Has something interesting and different—out of the mainstream of my life—happening most of the time
2. Takes reasonable care of myself, physically
3. Takes responsibility for doing something about the things that bother me rather than just being discontented
4. Has relationships with family and friends that are intimate, not just stuck in role playing

Step 4:   To take one step toward becoming the kind of person described in Step 3, I am willing to experiment with changing my coping progressions. Specifically, during the next two weeks (dates: *Sept. 15* to *Sept. 30*), I will substitute the following changes at the specified points in my typical coping process:

Instead of:	*I will:*
Remaining bored	Begin reading a new novel and attend the lecture on the Civil War that is being offered next Friday night.
Continuing to feel guilty about gaining weight	Begin a reasonable exercise plan that will involve taking at least two 45-minute walks, playing tennis once each week, and 15 minutes of calisthenics two times each week.
Staying socially stagnant	Invite my new business associate to lunch, and Jackie and I will invite my associate and his wife out to dinner.

continued

Instead of:	*I will:*
Withdrawing from my wife	Initiate a conversation with my wife at least twice each day; invite her out to lunch two times each week; ask her questions about how she is doing, rather than leaving it up to her to carry our conversations.

Step 5: During this program, I will ask the people indicated for the following forms of support and encouragement:

Support person:	*Specific request:*
Jackie, my wife	Encourage me to stick with this; say these words: "You deserve to feel better" and "You deserve to rest and eat when you want to"; don't nag about whether I'm sticking with this program; cook one of my favorite meals once each week as a family celebration of this new beginning.
Loretta and Rosana, my daughters	Be available for the family celebration meals. Come on a walk with me once each week—a time to talk.
Jim, my best friend	Come to the lecture on the Civil War with me next Friday; agree to do something other than play tennis on Saturday; have lunch and talk about this plan of change.

Step 6: To reward and motivate myself in this program, I will nurture myself each day in the following five ways:

continued

1. I will not do paperwork at home past 7:30 p.m.
2. I will make time to watch *The Andy Griffith Show* each day.
3. I will eat something that I really enjoy eating each day.
4. I will take time to read about high school teaching concepts.
5. I will stay in bed and relax every morning for 15 minutes after I wake up, rather than hitting the floor running as soon as the alarm sounds.

Step 7:   Two weeks from now, on (month *Sept.* day *30*), I will evaluate my progress by noting the following specifics about my style of living and coping during the preceding two weeks.

> Have I exercised as planned; talked more openly with my wife; invited my new acquaintance to lunch and he and his wife out for dinner; rewarded myself each day as planned; limited my work hours as planned; attended the lecture on the Civil War; begun reading a new novel; invited Jackie to lunch twice, and expressed interest in her during these lunches?

Step 8:   (To be completed at the time of the two-week evaluation.) Based on this two-week evaluation, I plan to change my immediate change program in the following ways, starting today:

_____

_____

_____

_____

CHANGE CONTRACT

With commitments to: (1) be honest with myself; (2) stay aware; (3) find the courage to change; and (4) be humble enough to go for good enough,

I _____ commit to the follow contract.

Step 1: I want to change the following about the way I am living or feeling:

_____

_____

Step 2: To do so, I need to remember that the feelings or behaviors specified in Step 1 occur as part of the following sequences (Please refer to Steps 1–11 from the "Identifying Coping Sequences That Backfire" exercise in this chapter):

_____

_____

Step 3: Instead of continuing the pattern specified in Step 2, I would like to be the kind of person who:

_____

_____

Step 4: To take one step toward becoming the kind of person described in Step 3, I am willing to experiment with changing my coping progressions. Specifically, during the next two weeks (dates: _____ to _____), I will substitute the following changes at the specified points in my typical coping process:

Instead of: *I will:*

_____   _____

Instead of:	*I will:*
_____	_____
_____	_____

Step 5:   During this program, I will ask the people indicated for the following forms of support and encouragement:
Support person: Specific request:

_____	_____
_____	_____
_____	_____
_____	_____

Step 6:   To reward and motivate myself in this program, I will nurture myself each day in the following ways:

1. _____

2. _____

3. _____

Step 7:   Two weeks from now, on month _____ day _____,
I will evaluate my progress by noting the following specifics about my style of living and coping during the preceding two weeks:

_____

_____

Step 8:   Based on this two-week evaluation, I plan to change my immediate change program in the following ways, starting today:

_____

_____

_____

The Challenge of Changing

Many of our clients begin healing their lives only once they face trauma: a health crisis; an ended romance; a career setback; the death of a loved one. We encourage you to begin this healing now. Pretend that the trauma has already slapped you into an awareness that this is no dress rehearsal; this is the only life that you have to live. Face the challenge to change in healthy ways, and you will enter the league of new heroes whose healthy relationships we would all like to emulate.

Chapter Eleven

Being a Dynamic Duo

In spite of seemingly insurmountable problems (with work, family, and individual needs) facing couples today, some people do manage to thrive where others are defeated. These are couples who live the Big Life but keep their relationships alive. They have recognized that intimacy is the key to stress hardiness, and cope in ways that are graceful, flexible, and obviously effective. They maintain high levels of passion and emotional closeness 15, 20, even 30 years after they say, "I do." When it comes to dealing with each other, the new Dynamic Duos teach us a valuable lesson: stress is inevitable, but struggling is optional.

As superachievers traveling through uncharted territory, we need each other's cooperation and connection. Social researchers have documented that an intimate marriage is a great boon to emotional and physical health and to work productivity. We have long known that supportive, intimate relationships can help you to better manage stress, improve your mood, and encourage healthy living. But we now know that a loving, supportive marriage can also increase work productivity and even decrease absenteeism from the job. Recent studies have shown that employees who have the benefit of helping behaviors and satisfaction in their marriages have fewer psychosomatic symptoms, less depression, and greater satisfaction with their jobs, even when the job is highly stressful. Marital difficulties, on the other hand, seem to contribute to increased job turnover, general career dissatisfaction, and burnout. To work as a team, we must regularly pause to ask our partners questions that will keep us on course. Dynamic Duos repeatedly ask themselves the following questions.

Does Our Contract Need Updating?

We have identified six distinct relationship patterns that supercouples employ. These patterns are shaped by the ways that couples originally contract their respective roles and in the ways that high-powered coping is expressed as they manage their Big Life.

These patterns are not mutually exclusive, nor do they encompass every possibility, since each couple has unique styles, strengths, and weaknesses. However, familiarizing yourself with these patterns will probably shed light on what's happening in your relationship.

The Good Mother/Bad Boy

Here, an ambitious, career-oriented man and a nurturing *good mother* find each other. He goes to work, she creates a life. The wife is supposed to nurture her husband so that his drive is kept in check; she becomes the family stress absorber.

During the couple's early child-rearing years, this arrangement works because there's an appreciation for each partner's contribution. The wife takes pride in her caretaking role. The husband basks in his position of respect and power—the marriage revolves around his professional demands, emotional needs, fatigue, preferences, and priorities. Both spouses hope that the wife's infinite love and patience will provide him with peace and contentment and counter-balance his drive. They both assume that once he reaches his goals, he'll relax and join her in a more nurturing lifestyle.

But the husband doesn't change, and the couple drifts into living separate lives. She begins to question whether her nurturing and stress absorption may be promoting the very thing that hurts their intimacy—his driven way of living. At the same time, the husband becomes bored with his unexciting wife. Limited by the roles she has been assigned and assumed, she is no longer clearly visible to him. She, in turn, feels misunderstood, so she builds a life that excludes him. When not attending to her kids' needs, she pursues interests that don't involve her partner. Meanwhile, he continues to build a life outside the home, and his self-focused style further disconnects him from his spouse. Depleted, the wife becomes angry and hurt that her husband no longer values her contribution. And he is left to wonder where his all-nurturing wife went.

Both partners in this pattern become candidates for extramarital affairs. He is attracted to women who seem more exciting than his wife. She is attracted to men who notice and affirm her, as her husband used to do.

Pleasing Others, Even If It Kills Me or Them

This relationship revolves around a woman who wants to be all things to all people. She may have a career, a leadership role in her community, or an otherwise busy life, but she insists on being a hands-on caretaker. Her underlying hope is that her spouse will validate, applaud, and nurture her. But her husband gets lost in his own Big Life and tends to forget how high-powered she is. His respect is important to her, and when she loses it her vibrancy suffers.

A variation of this scenario is one in which a high-powered woman's excessive need for validation and control drives the relationship and family life. She must have perfect children, recognition of her talents and work, a thriving social life, and a successful spouse. She is often previously a career woman who now manages her family with the same fervor she did her career. She overmonitors and prods her children, becomes consumed with volunteer work, and pushes her husband to be more ambitious. The effect? Her loved ones begin to avoid her and her husband begins to resent her drivenness.

These couples settle into exhaustion, lack of validation, and loss of connection.

Ready, Set, Go!

We have discussed these couples the most. Two exceptionally competitive hard-drivers marry with the hope that they will stimulate each other and have it all. However, they share an underlying wish: that one will teach the other to calm down and settle for a smaller, more traditional life. Instead, they cooperate in creating ultrabig lives, then resent the complexity. Their relationship moves from high-energy and stimulation to a long-suffering endurance contest. They compete over everything: Who can parent best, who can make the most money, whose headache is worse. As they go on, they grow tired of struggling.

These are the folks who most often threaten to downscale their lives, but who seldom do it. They lament, "We should sell all of this stuff, move to the shore, and open a little shop." They both know, however, that if they did this, they would make the little shop a successful business and franchise it.

Each partner in this pattern longs for a taste of the more traditional gender treatment from the other. *He* wants *her* to treat him in ways that affirm his masculinity. *She* wants *him* to treat her in ways that affirm her femininity. They grow tired of the competition, the flow-charts that organize their Big Life, and the exhaustion that bores them in their bedroom.

Chaotic Desperation

These marriages revolve around the chaos that comes from hot-reacting partners. The spouses believe they can love the anger away; both partners hope that the hot reactors will outgrow their outbursts. The spouses are lifelines of nurturing and calm that keep the hot reactors in reasonable balance. In these relationships, hot reactors believe they've finally found a place of unconditional love.

Unfortunately, both partners end up disillusioned and feeling abandoned. Spouses grow tired of constantly running interference to keep the hot reactors from flaring. Hot reactors get frustrated and target more anger at their spouses. Given that emotions are contagious, the spouses eventually begin to show more irritation and defensiveness, no matter how nurturing and calm they may have originally been. Mismanaged anger, bitterness, and defensiveness fill these marriages and homes. Threatened or real periods of separation are juxtaposed with brief periods of reconciliation that end with another outburst.

The Island Man or Woman

This pattern is the flip side of the chaotic desperation marriage. Here, the relationship revolves around an emotionally distant, high-powered partner who feels uncomfortable with intimate connection. These are *island* folks who live for inordinate amounts of time in the superperson leg of the high-powered triad. Their spouses are anchors for their relationships during the storms of shame and depression that living cut-off from emotional awareness inevitably produces. The island partners hope that their loving mates will always be there for them—from a distance. Island partners are uncomfortable if their spouses get too close or drift too far away. The anchoring partners hope that eventually their spouses will leave their islands and comfortably participate in love.

These couples get stuck in an exaggerated version of the pursuer-distancer dance. The risk here is that both partners will settle into a life of quiet desperation, never finding a comfortable way of living together, but fearing what will happen to the island partners if they part.

Too Mellow to Admit It

Having come of age in the 60s and 70s, these couples aspire to mellow, centered lives. Yet, they create the Big Life that makes a laid-back lifestyle impossible. They try to keep their ambitiousness, competitiveness, and drivenness a secret by filling their lives with mellow activities, such as the symphony and the opera. Their secret? They want to leave at intermission, go home, and do some paperwork.

Here, the underlying contract is each partner's willingness to perpetuate the other's laid-back and mellow facade. They recoil when their partners shame them for being competitive, ambitious, rushed, or hostile. These partners are especially plagued by the narcissistic expectation that in relationships, they are supposed to have it all without having to work too strenuously to get it.

These couples tend to bail out when the going gets rough: They move on to find new relationships that stimulate them with the bliss of beginnings, only to once again flounder when these relationships move beyond the stage of infatuation.

What Are We Struggling About?

In *Getting The Love You Want*, author Harville Hendrix reminds us that in a long-term relationship, romantic love always gives way to disillusionment and struggles to change each other. These struggles do not signal a bad relationship; they come with a rough stretch in the road of your journey together. You know your relationship needs updating if you find yourself struggling to change your partner into the ideal mate you thought your partner would be when you first met.

Heart Illness and Intimacy: How Caring Relationships Aid Recovery, outlines the various ways that couples struggle to change each other:

They lament, "You promised":   "You would work less once we had children." "You would stop associating with those friends once we moved." "You would put some distance between you and your family once we married."

They may accuse, "You've changed":   "Why do you make such a big deal of this? You knew who I was when we got together. I'm just being me; *you've* changed."

They may plead, "For the sake of":   "For the sake of your health, why don't you slow down." "For the sake of our children, why don't you learn to control your temper." "For God's sake, just change into what I always thought you would become!"

The struggle grows tiring as neither gives in to the other's requests for change. The pursuer-distancer dance intensifies. Frustration with the struggle eventually leads to disillusionment about the way the marriage turned out. Silently or aloud, a haunting question is considered: "Maybe we got married for more wrong reasons than right reasons. Since this is the only life I have to live, maybe I don't want to spend it struggling with you about something so basic as _____." (Fill in the blank: sex, stress, parenting, or whatever you struggle to change about your partner.)

Differentiation

Dynamic Duos move beyond their struggling by accepting their equally limited capacities to change the other. They accept that the marriage can soothe some pains or fulfill some needs, but that they each have feelings of aloneness, or emptiness, or conflict that their spouses cannot soothe. But unlike the Dynamic Duos, many of us drift into feeling alone and abandoned by our true love who served as everything we needed when we were in Bliss City.

At this point the illusions of love start to peel away. What originally attracted you to your partner starts to repel you; the roles that you originally assumed with such ease begin to tire you. We call this the *before marriage/after marriage shuffle*. It goes like this:

BEFORE MARRIAGE	AFTER MARRIAGE
We are soul-mates. We think the same thoughts.	Don't you ever have an original thought? Leave my thoughts alone.
You're so good for me. You make me do the right things.	You are boring me to death. I wanna have some fun!
You're so organized; it makes me feel safe.	Why don't you loosen up!
I love how sensitive you are. That's rare in a man.	What a wimp. I want a real man.
Let me take care of you, till death do us part.	Do I look like your mother? Pick up your own damn socks! I am not your mother.

This is a crucial stage in a relationship, and it is often misunderstood. It is here that so many couples bolt from each other as a way of blurring their confrontation with their own innermost fear: that we must learn to take responsibility for ourselves. The distraction of a new romance or a new quest allows the illusion that the real problem was that soon-to-be-ex mate, not ourselves.

In truth, these struggles signal that you are growing, not dying. What you do next determines the outcome of the relationship. Couples who do not run from each other have the opportunity to create a more mature and enduring love; one that can last a lifetime.

Using Our Good Stuff to Make It Better

The new Dynamic Duos create healing partnerships. They go through the same stages all long-term relationships go through, but they bear through their fear of differentiating and calm their power struggles as they get more honest and realistic. They also use their relationships to help manage their Big Life. Partners muster the courage to confront their relationship narcissism and the effects it is having on others. By working together to manage the situations, processes, and relationships that fill their lives, they create a life territory that gives their romance a lasting chance.

Perhaps most important, Dynamic Duos keep the perspective that marriage is a journey toward good enough. That doesn't mean they settle for something less than passionate. It means they understand and accept that the intoxication couples feel early on is only one stage in the journey. Once the infatuation goes, rather than growing stagnant and settling into a lifetime of struggling, these couples create alliances that are highly caring, loving, and warm. They do this by working together to renegotiate the relationship contract that organizes how they act and how they perceive each other. In short, they clarify their psychological boundaries.

Are We in the Right Dance Spaces?

A scene from the movie *Dirty Dancing* points out the importance of clear boundaries in creating relationship teamwork. Patrick Swayze was charged with the task of teaching novice Jennifer Gray an intricate dance. After a number of frustrating tries, he clarified: "Look. This is *my* dance space (signalling around himself with his arms). Here is *your* dance space (signalling around his partner with his arms). Stay in *your* dance space."

Clarifying your boundaries will move you beyond the misguided notion that the two of you together will make one whole person and will help you to dance cooperatively as you accomplish BEST.

Psychological boundaries encompass two things: (1) Whether we are clear with ourselves about what we think, feel, need, and want; and (2) how we manage ourselves vis-a-vis others.

Clarifying boundaries is a survival skill, both for individuals and for couples. Without clear boundaries, we get lost struggling with each other and we fail to adequately protect our family from outside influences. We also compromise our main lever against burnout—intimacy.

The concepts from Ian Stewart and Vann Joines' *TA Today; A New Introduction to Transactional Analysis* are quite helpful in understanding boundaries. The authors explain how, early in life, we formulate convictions about ourselves and the people around us that are likely to stay with us for a lifetime. These convictions, called *life positions*, represent fundamental stances we take up about the essential values we perceive in ourselves and others. Our life positions can be summarized with four statements about self and others that have obvious boundary implications:

- I'm OK, You're OK;
- I'm Not OK, You're OK;

- I'm OK, You're Not OK;
- I'm Not OK, You're Not OK.

Each of us shifts among these positions at different times in our lives. Our life positions lead us to develop one of three types of boundary operations: too porous, too rigid, or healthily semiporous.

Too-Porous Boundaries

If we discount ourselves, we will develop overly porous boundaries. We become unclear about our own internal experience and we have difficulty accepting the validity of our thoughts, feelings, needs, and wants.

I'm Not OK, You're OK: We discount ourselves in deference to what others think or want from us. We drive ourselves with efforts to please others or to be perfect enough in others' eyes to gain value. Because we do not set appropriate limits, relationships prove to be exhausting and invasive. We avoid them by drifting into depression or illness, which is a misguided way of saying the no we dare not utter verbally, given how we discount our own rights.

Example: You arrive home frazzled. As soon as you enter your house, your daughter clamors, "I hate all my clothes! I've been waiting for you to take me to the mall. I don't have anything to wear tomorrow. Can we go right now?"

I'm Not OK, You're OK *response: "I'm sorry. I should have known you would want something new to wear tomorrow." With a sigh, you rush off with her, quietly going more numb to block your exhaustion and irritation.*

Too-Rigid Boundaries

Some people defend themselves by developing overly rigid boundaries.

I'm OK, You're Not OK: These folks learned that living for them-selves was a safer bet than being vulnerable to others. But their sense of self is brittle and masks underlying insecurities and fears born of experiences with others that hurt them.

Life in this life position involves getting rid of others because you don't trust their good intentions. You might do so by reminding your-self to be careful, don't trust, and don't become involved. Rather, you selectively perceive others' flaws, find ways to disagree with them, show anger and irritation, or generally act in ways that intimidate or alienate. Or, you might simply keep your physical distance. Here, isolating yourself becomes a lifestyle. You justify your stance by remaining angry or suspicious. Others cooperate by avoiding you and your barbs.

Example: You and your partner are leaving your partner's office Christmas party, where you were introduced to the two new associ-ates your partner has been talking about for months.

I'm OK, You're Not OK *response:*   *"Well those two seem like head cases to me. He's obviously a fool, and she's a hypocrite. Did you notice that she contradicted herself about what she did at her last job? I don't see what you like about those people. In fact, your office seems to attract people who are caught up in one form of B-S or another."*

The Terrible Too's: Too Porous and Too Rigid Boundaries

I'm Not OK, You're Not OK: If you ascribe this life position to your-self, others probably describe you as passive/aggressive. Your com-plaining or suffering suggest to others that you need their input or help. But your distrust, coupled with your basic discounting of your right to be happy, leads to the habit of yes-but. Whatever others sug-gest or try to do to help you out is acknowledged but ineffective. Eventually others tire of trying to help you, and they go away. You then are left with confirmation of your life position: "I knew I couldn't trust others to understand; they are Not OK."

Example: You complain, "We just don't make love often enough. It's not like it used to be." Later, your partner approaches you romantically.

I'm Not OK, You're Not OK *response: You passively participate but clearly do not enjoy. Or, even more blatantly, you say: "You know that I always want to make love, but now it's too late. Why did you have to wait until now to approach me? This just makes it worse."*

The Good News: Semipermeable Boundaries

Fortunately, a healthy alternative does exist if we establish semipermeable boundaries that are firm enough to protect our space yet porous enough to let information, people, and ideas in.

I'm OK, You're OK: Bolstered with a life position that reassures that both they and others are trustworthy and valuable, these people are able to take care of themselves and participate in healthy relationships. They are able to negotiate a comfortable balance between closeness and distance without resorting to negative emotional dramas with others.

These people are reasonably clear about what they think, feel, need, or want and are trusting enough to be interested in the same about others. They know how to say "Yes, come in and let's get to know each other." But they also know how to say "No thanks; that's not me."

Example: Your daughter clamors for you to take her to the mall right now.
I'm OK, You're OK *response: "I'm sorry you don't like what you have to wear. But I'm not willing to go to the mall tonight; I'm bushed. If you'd like, I will help you look through your closet and choose something that will be good enough for tomorrow."*

Example: You and your partner leave your partner's office party.
I'm OK, You're OK *response: "Well, I wasn't crazy about those two new associates, but I don't know them like you do. Help me understand more about what they are like."*

Example: Your partner approaches you after you have complained about your sex life.

I'm OK, You're OK response: *"That's a nice invitation. I appreci-ate that we can always talk about things, even the hard stuff. I love making love to you. But I'm really tired right now. How about if we have a date tomorrow morning?"*

None of us spends all of our time acting in the ways described in any one of these life positions. We bounce back and forth, even though we have a favorite position where we spend most of our time. It is helpful to note your tendencies.

WHEN, WHERE, AND HOW DO I GO?

In your journal, answer the following questions.

1. Which life position do you naturally drift to?
2. What circumstances lead to your getting into each life position?
3. Are you more likely to assume certain life positions with certain people?
4. What do you typically do and say and how do you typically feel when you are in each life position?

Are You Fighting the Right Fight?

We believe that intimacy is a key to wellness and happiness. The Big Life is filled with challenges, but none is more important than fight-ing to keep your intimacy alive.

If you took a videotape of an alive, highly passionate couple for one year and compared it to a similar video of a stale, struggling couple, certain differences would be apparent. We have found ten characteristics necessary to make Dynamic Duos.

Develop and Maintain a Relationship Work Ethic

"Loving is not for the weak." This cautioning from Dr. David Schnarch shows that lifelong romance takes courage and work.

Couples who expect love and romance to grow naturally fail. The truth is that few things in life are as complicated as an intimate relationship. The new Dynamic Duos accept the need to work on their relationships constantly, and they use their considerable energies to get through periods that require extra effort. It is far easier to have a half-baked, lukewarm, functional-but-not-very-intimate relationship. Intimate relationships take sustained effort.

Be Humble

No matter how exceptional you might be as individuals or as a couple, you won't be the exception to the rules that apply to relationships. Respecting the factors that help or hinder relationships can safeguard your family. Remember:

- *Think team.* What will this choice on my part (to work overtime, to accept a transfer, to go back to work, to quit working) do to the people I love?
- *Protect the boundaries that separate your marriage and your family from the rest of the world.* This might mean refusing to work or worry on certain days or nights. It might mean saying no to relatives who want more of you than you have time or energy to give. It might mean saying no to your own children to protect time with your spouse.
- *Accept that in real life, good enough is as perfect as it gets.* Dynamic Duos accept that sacrifices and compromises have to be made. To have reasonable balance, you may have to settle for a job rather than pursuing a career. You may have to limit how many children you have, to quiet the drama about whether you can adequately provide for your family. Most of all, you will have to accept that there is not time enough in this chapter of life to do and be all that you might aspire to.

Communicate

Most high-powered couples spend relatively little time awake, in each other's presence, and paying attention. This is one of the main reasons that our journey through the new normal so often gets clouded. Unless we constantly communicate, signalling to our partners where we are and hearing from them a recognizable signal in turn, we will lose each other along the way. Volumes have been written on communication strategies, but all this boils down to one key point:

> Control the situations and processes of your Big Life so that you can give your relationship and your romance a chance to grow.

Protect your communication-generating rituals. Dynamic Duos regularly create time to be alone with each other. It really doesn't seem to matter much how they go about making that happen; what matters is that they continue to do it. They don't call what they do a *communication-generating ritual*, but that's the purpose it serves. No matter how busy, they save time for each other. Some ideas for creating together time include:

- Taking a planned night off each week
- Taking a walk together several times each week
- Going out to breakfast alone once each week
- Sitting together for 15 minutes each day and visiting without any other distractions.

Of course, how you deal with each other during such times is crucial, too. Some high-powered couples have magnificent communication skills, but lousy communication with each other. They settle into communicating by phone, rather than in person; by notes, rather than eye-to-eye; in a rush, rather than with each other's full attention; when exhausted or stressed, rather than when refreshed and relaxed.

Help Each Other Manage Anger

Anger is one of the most prevalent by-products of the Big Life. Anger management is a real test of BEST. Dynamic Duos help each other take responsibility for breaking the cycle in which hostile, cynical attitudes fuel unpleasant emotions, leading to aggressive behaviors that stress others and create more tension. They do this by helping each other control what happens next when one or both of them gets angry. Six strategies are important in helping each other manage anger.

- Recognize that anger signals frustration of some underlying need, and try to figure out what that need might be.
- Avoid fueling anger with judgments that you are being done an injustice or that your stress is due to someone's purposefully behaving in an incompetent way.
- Don't confuse assertion with aggression. Pay particular attention to six aspects of your communication style: (1) Verbal behaviors; (2) nonverbal sounds; (3) voice quality, tone, and volume; (4) hand and arm gestures; (5) facial expressions; and (6) body movements.
- Respect your differences. Some hard-driving people have overreactive flight-or-fight reactions and impoverished calming reactions. If this describes you, it is crucial that you pay attention to the basics in managing stress. Beware of stimulants like caffeine, nicotine, and simple sugars. Also remember that doing and thinking more than one thing at once activates a stress response. Before trying to discuss a problem with your partner, take a break to clear your mind and wash stress out of your body with exercise or relaxation. If you are losing control of your temper during a discussion, call time out but state your commitment to returning to finish the discussion once you calm down.

If it is your partner who is the hot reactor, give him or her time to cool down before pushing for resolution of your conflict. Choosing to take a break in your discussions is not the same as denying that a problem exists. It is always wisest to strike while the iron is warm, not hot.

- Deal with one issue at a time. Don't let anger about one issue lead you into showering the other person with a cascade of issues. Remember that any issue important enough to make you angry deserves its own discussion. If a new issue surfaces during your conflict, flag it as a topic to address later.

- Start early. Notice subtle signs that anger or irritation is building. If you are harboring these feelings, express them before they build too much. If you sense that your partner is growing upset, offer to help, to simply listen, or to discuss the issue at hand. In this way, you can disrupt the domino progressions that otherwise lead to angry outbursts.

- Negotiate. Managing anger is about negotiating new outcomes to problem situations. Successful negotiation involves separating the person from the problem being addressed, and, while holding to your own most important issues, calming the person.

> Stroke your partner and demonstrate a leap of faith that you will resolve the problem.
>
> Validate your partner's perceptions, even if you have a different perspective.
>
> Don't blame your partner or turn a manageable problem into a catastrophe.
>
> Emphasize where you agree.
>
> Apologize. Remember: Apologizing is not the same as accepting blame; it's a statement of regret that you are having this conflict.
>
> Don't lock into positions; clarify your underlying issues, and respond to these.

Declare Your Commitment, Then Do It Again, and Again, and. . . .

"In this age of 'lite' everything—lite beer, lite ice cream, lite crackers—we somehow are getting lulled into pretending that there is an option to have a 'lite intimate marriage'." Nothing could be further from true. Long-range intimacy requires repeated declarations of commitment to your partner. This means many things, most of which are variations of a single theme:

Commitment is not what you say; it's how you act.

Committed couples protect the boundaries around their relationships. They share more secrets with each other than they do with others. They make decisions with deference to the impact that the decisions will have on their partnerships. They also commit to keeping up with each others' growth.

Give Each Other Permission to Change

It is fascinating to note how much more couples know about each other early in their relationship than they do once they've been together for years. The reason? We stop paying attention.

Remember: If you aren't learning something new about each other every week or two, you simply aren't paying close enough attention.

Bored couples fail to update the lenses through which they view each other. They act as though the roles they assigned and assumed early in the relationship will remain forever comfortable.

Worse yet, struggling couples act as though a partner's changing is a double cross. This is because change by one partner always requires the other to change, too, and this can be stressful. Remember, we are creatures of habit: We lock in perspectives on each other, and assign and assume roles in the relationship that allow us to fit together comfortably. In doing this, each of us puts certain aspects of our selves on the shelf, at least temporarily.

But eventually we are compelled to take these parts of ourselves off the shelf and incorporate them into our lives. This push for integration of formerly split-off parts of ourselves leads us to feel as though we are outgrowing, or growing tired of, the roles that have organized our relationships thus far. When this happens, we face the stress of having to reorganize our relationships in reaction to our individual changes.

Dynamic Duos accept that the stress of growing is an inevitable part of being married, and they are careful not to sabotage each other. When you struggle with your own growing pains, you need to nurture each other more than ever.

Hold yourselves accountable for keeping up with each others' dreams, fears, hopes, regrets, wishes, and fantasies. We continue to trust people who know us and validate us.

Have Fun!

We fall in love with people who make us laugh. We stay in love with those who make us feel safe enough to come out to play. Dynamic Duos make playing together a priority. And they continue to put creative energy into making themselves playful and creating relationships that regularly feel like recess.

Make Yourself Trustworthy

When it comes to building trust, the way we deal with each other day to day is more important than single events. We trust people who validate us. We learn to distrust those who act as though our relationship is a competition over who is right. Dynamic Duos act as though each of them has thoughts, impressions, and preferences that make sense, even if their opinions or needs differ. They know their partner's perceptions will always contain at least a few truths, even if they only involve that partner's impressions. Dynamic Duos validate those truths before adding their perspectives to the discussion.

Forgive

We high-powered types are hard on ourselves and on each other. We make many mistakes along our life journey. If our passion and love are to survive, we must learn how to forgive. We need to regularly forgive ourselves and each other.

Holding onto resentments is a way of blocking intimacy. It will only assure that no matter how hard you otherwise work at it, your relationship will not grow.

Practice the wisdom of the proverb: "Unforgiven hurt is like caressing a hot ember that has been placed in your hand." Cast it aside, and do what you can to heal the wound in the relationship, even if you did not cause it.

It is also important to forgive each other for the sheer stress and fatigue caused by our Big Lives. Be compassionate about the fact that neither of you intended to hurt the other as you set out on this journey. The pain that comes needs to be soothed by forgiving, not irritated by resenting.

Cherish

The most fundamental ingredient in the intimacy formula is cherishing each other. It's not enough to cooperate in creating or managing the Big Life. Self-sacrifice at the expense of your own happiness or well-being is not enough. It certainly isn't enough to bear through your pain but end up drained and joyless while taking care of your commitments.

We need to celebrate each other's presence. If we don't give our partners admiration, acknowledgement, applause, the benefit of the doubt, appreciation, encouragement, and the message, "I'm happy that you are here with me now," where will they receive these gifts? Remember our prior advice: Be generous; be gracious.

Is it really possible to move beyond the Supercouple Syndrome that characterizes life in the new normal? The thousands of Dynamic Duos we have known prove that the answer to this question is a resounding yes! By supporting each other while each takes responsibility for managing hurry sickness and hard-driving coping styles, Dynamic Duos manage to control the effect that their Big Life has on their marriage and family.

There are no perfect relationships. But Dynamic Duos represent an evolutionary step in marriage. They are the new male and female heroes: people who understand that men, women, work, and family are integrally interrelated, and who do what they can to help each other manage the juggling act of our day.

Videos, Audiotapes, and Books by Wayne and Mary Sotile

Videos

High-Powered Relationships: How to Keep the Flame Alive!

This 90-minute video featuring Dr. Wayne Sotile is chock full of fresh humor and remarkable insights about today's relationships. It is a perfect gift for loved ones or coworkers. Topics include:

• Men and women and stress resistance
• The stages of a couple's journey
• Seven characteristics of a high-passion marriage
• How to make your workplace stress resistant
• The work/family balancing act: thriving, not just surviving

Coping with Heart Illness

This series of three, 90-minute videotapes featuring Dr. Wayne Sotile examines the psychological side of living with heart illness. Separate tapes examine patient issues, couple issues, and family issues. Learn how to: Cope with depression; manage emotions; cope with sexual fears after illness; talk about illness with children and grandchildren; and create family teamwork in making lifestyle changes.

Audiotapes

The BEST Model for Balancing Work and Family

These three, 60-minute audiotapes featuring Wayne and Mary Sotile can change your relationships forever. Based on their *BEating Stress Together* model, these tapes teach you how to: Control yourself during uncontrollable times; keep passion alive amid your Big Life; and diagnose and manage your personality-based stress reactions.

Other Books

The Medical Marriage: A Couple's Survival Guide

Heart Illness and Intimacy: How Caring Relationships Aid Recovery

To order any of these materials or to inquire about the Sotiles' availability to speak to your organization, please write, FAX or call:

Sotile Psychological Associates
1396 Old Mill Circle
Winston-Salem, NC 27103

Phone: 910-765-3032 or 1-888-629-2313   FAX: 910-760-6977
(Between 9:00 a.m. and 5:00 p.m., EST)

Chapter Notes

Chapter 2

9 These coping styles were originally referred to as a single syndrome, termed *Type A behavior pattern* (TYABP). The prevailing notion is that TYABP exists on a continuum ranging from some individuals exhibiting singular Type A coping characteristics to some who evidence multiple Type A characteristics in their coping style. See S. G. Haynes and K. A. Matthews (1988). Review and methodologic critique of recent studies on Type A behavior and cardiovascular disease. *Annals of Behavior Medicine*, 10, 47–59; V. X. Helgeson (1989). The origin, development, and current state of the literature on Type A behavior. *Journal of Cardiovascular Nursing*, 3(2), 59–73.

11 This list was adapted from W. M. Sotile and M. O. Sotile (1996). *The medical marriage: A couple's survival guide.* (New York: Birch Lane Press).

11 This scale was originally published in *The Medical Marriage* as "Type A Behavior: How Do You Compare?".

12 For discussion of vital exhaustion, see P. R. J. Falger, E. G. W. Schouten, and A. W. Appels (April 27–30, 1988). Relation-

ships between age, Type A behavior, life changes over the life-span, vital exhaustion, and first myocardial infarction: A case-referent study. *Proceedings of the Society of Behavioral Medicine* (Boston, M.A.), 26.

17   Our *BEating Stress Together* model is an expansion of our model for stress hardiness as applied to individuals, called *Effective Emotional Management.* See Sotile and Sotile, *The medical marriage,* and W. M. Sotile (1996). *Psychosocial interventions for cardiopulmonary patients: A guide for health professionals.* (Champaign, IL: Human Kinetics).

17   For a thorough discussion of the concept of stress hardiness, see S. C. Kobasa (1982). Commitment and coping in stress resistance among lawyers. *Journal of Personality and Social Psychology,* 42, 707–17; *Idem* (1982). The hardy personality: Toward a social psychology theory of stress and health. In B.S. Sanders and J. Suls (Eds.), *Social psychology of health and illness.* (Hillsdale, NJ: Erlbaum); S. C. Kobasa, S. R. Maddi, and S. Kahn (1982). Hardiness and and health: A prospective study. *Journal of Personality and Social Psychology,* 42, 168–72; S. C. Kobasa (September 1984). How much stress can you survive? *American Health,* 3, 64–77; S. R. Maddi and S. C. Kobasa (1984). *The hardy executive: Health under stress.* (Homewood, IL: Dow Jones-Irwin); M. Pines (December 1980). Psychological hardiness: The role of challenge in health. *Psychology Today,* 34–44; F. Walsh (1996). The concept of family resilience: Crisis and challenge. *Family Process,* 35(3), 261–81.

Chapter 3

21   Michele Ritterman (1995). Stopping the clock. *Family Therapy Networker,* 19(1), 45–51. Quote from p. 46.

22   R. Todd Erkel (1995). Time shifting. *Family Therapy Networker,* 19(1), 33–39. Quote from p. 39.

22 Ritterman, Stopping the clock, 46.

22 Michael Ventura (1995). The age of interruption. *Family Therapy Networker,* 19(1), 18–32.

22 Ritterman, Stopping the clock, 46.

23 Vince Bielski (1996). Our magnificent obsession. *Family Therapy Networker,* 29(2), 22–35.

23 Mark McCormick (1991). *The 110% solution.* New York: Bantam.

23 T. Peters and N. Austin (1985). *A passion for excellence.* (New York: Warner Books), 496.

24 Sally Weiner (March 12, 1990). Stop whining and get back to work. *Fortune,* 49–50.

24 Juliet Schor (1992). *The overworked American: The unexpected decline of leisure.* (New York: Basic Books).

24 This study was discussed in Barbara Bailey Reinhold (1996). *Toxic work.* (New York: Dutton).

26 Jaine M. Carter and James D. Carter (1995). *He works/she works™: Successful strategies for working couples.* (New York: AMACOM).

31 For seminal work with Type A behavior pattern, see M. Friedman and D. Ulmer (1984). *Treating Type A behavior and your heart.* (New York: Alfred A. Knopf).

31 See C. E. Thoresen and K. G. Low (1990). Women and Type A behavior pattern: Review and commentary. In M. J. Strube (Ed.), Type A behavior. *Journal of Social Behavior and Personality,* 5(1) [special issue], 117–33; G. E. Moss et al. (1986). Demographic correlates of 51 assessments of Type A behavior. *Psychosomatic Medicine,* 4, 564–674; L. J. Baker et al. (1984). Type A behavior in women: A review. *Health Psychology,* 3, 477–97.

31 This triad represents our modification of a similar concept originally proposed by Virginia Ann Price in her seminal work with Type A individuals. Price suggests that Type As vacillate through the roles of superperson, depressed person, and angry

person. See V. A. Price (1982). *Type A behavior pattern: A model for research and practice.* (New York: Academic Press).

31   See S. Yogev (1982). Are professional women overworked? Objective versus subjective perception of role loads. *Journal of Occupational Psychology, 55,* 165–69.

32   See E. R. Greenglass (1990). Type A behavior, career aspirations, and role conflict in professional women. In M. J. Strube (Ed.), Type A behavior, 319. For research on Type As tendencies to suppress negative feeling states, see C. S. Carver, A. E. Coleman, and D. C. Glass (1976). The coronary-prone behavior pattern and the suppression of fatigue on a treadmill test. *Journal of Personality and Social Psychology, 33,* 460–66; K. A. Matthews (1982). Psychological perspectives on the Type A behavior pattern. *Psychological Bulletin, 91,* 293–323.

32   Sam Osherson (1992). *Wrestling with love: How men struggle with intimacy, with women, children, parents, and each other.* (New York: Fawcett Columbine).

33   Sotile and Sotile, *The medical marriage.*

34   Reinhold, *Toxic work,* 67. Summarizing research by M. Frankenhauser (1996). Psychobiological aspects of life stress. In S. Levine and U. Holger (Eds.), *Coping and health.* (New York: Plenum), 203–23.

Chapter 4

36   See Carol Gilligan (1982). *In a different voice.* (Cambridge: Harvard University Press); Nancy Chodorow (1978). *The reproduction of mothering.* (Berkeley: University of California Press).

37   For discussion of the developmental crossover phenomenon, see David Gutman (1987). *Reclaimed powers: Toward a new psychology of men and women in later life.* (New York: Basic Books).

38   Ventura, The age of interruption.

38   Sotile and Sotile, *The medical marriage.*

38   See B. K. Houston and K. E. Kelly (1987). Type A behavior in housewives: Relation to work, marital adjustment, stress, tension, health, fear-of-failure and self-esteem. *Journal of Psychosomatic Research*, 31, 55–61; C. E. Thoresen and K. G. Low (1990). Women and the Type A behavior pattern: Review and commentary. In M. J. Strube (Ed.), Type A behavior.

38   For reviews of discussions of high-powered coping and women, see M. J. Davidson, C. L. Cooper, and D. Chamberlain (1980). Type A coronary-prone behavior and stress in senior female managers and administrators. *Journal of Occupational Medicine*, 22, 801–05; M. J. Dearborn and J. E. Hastings (1987). Type A personality as a mediator of stress and strain in employed women. *Journal of Human Stress*, 13, 53–60; E. DeGregorio and C. Carver (1980). Type A behavior pattern, sex role orientation, and psychological adjustment. *Journal of Personality and Social Psychology*, 39, 286–93; S. Haynes and M. Feinleib (1980). Women, work and coronary heart disease: Prospective findings from the Framingham Heart Study. *American Journal of Public Health*, 70, 133–41; Houston and Kelly (1987). Type A behavior in housewives; Thoresen and Low (1990). Women and the Type A behavior pattern. In M. J. Strube (Ed.), Type A behavior.

39   See DeGregorio and Carver. Type A behavior pattern.

39   See Tina Adler (July 1993). Stress from work, home hits men, women equally. *The APA Monitor*, 24(7), 11–14. See especially p. 11. See also Rosalind Barnett and Caryl Rivers (1996). *She works/He works: How two-income families are happier, healthier, and better off.* San Francisco: Harper.

40   Margaret Mead, as quoted in Men: Tomorrow's second sex. *The Economist*, (September 28, 1996), 23–26.

40   Cited in Reinhold, *Toxic work.*

41   Carter and Carter, *He works/she works™*; Arlie Hochschild (1989). *The second shift.* (New York: Avon Books).

41   *The Economist.* Men: Tomorrow's second sex.

42   Ibid., 25.

44   Percentage of dual career couples from 1980–1988. In Work and family today: 100 key statistics. *The BNA Special Report Series on Work Work and Family,* no. 41 (May 1991), 25.

44   Barnett and Rivers, *She works/he works.*

44   Carter and Carter, *He works/she works™.*

45   Ellen H. Parlapiano and Patricia Cobe (1996). *Mompreneurs: A mother's practical step-by-step guide to work-at-home success.* (New York: Berkley Publishing Group).

45   Carter and Carter, *He works/She works™.*

Chapter 5

49   Struggles with emptiness are also part of the pursuer/distancer dance. See T. F. Fogarty (1976). On emptiness and closeness: Part I. *The Family,* 3, 3–12; *Idem* (1976). On emptiness and closeness: Part II. *The Family,* 3, 39–48.

50   For a thorough discussion of the concept of attempted solutions, see S. Osherson and S. Krugman (1990). Men, shame, and psychotherapy. In Robert Meth and Robert Pasic (1990). *Men in therapy: The challenge of change.* (New York: Guilford). Various "hypermasculine postures" were outlined in Augustus Napier (1991). The new male hero. *Journal of Marriage and Family,* 17(1), 30–41.

53   Osherson, *Wrestling with love,* 179.

53   Ibid., 56.

56   Carter and Carter, *He works/she works™,* 21.

57 M. A. Mason (September 1988). The equality trap. *Working Mother*, 38. Also see Nancy R. Gibbs (June 28, 1993). Bring up father. *Time*, 53–56.

57 From M. McGoldrick, C. Anderson, and F. Walsh (1989). *Women in families*. (New York: W. W. Norton).

57 This study was conducted by the Family and Work Institute and reported in R. Taffel (September/October 1994). The power of two. *Family Therapy Networker*, 18(5), 44–55.

57 Reported in Carter and Carter, *He works/She works™*.

59 See A. Napier (1988). *The fragile bond: In search of an equal, intimate and enduring marriage*. (New York: Harper & Row).

61 Carter and Carter, *He works/she works™*, 174.

67 Betsy Morris (September 18, 1995). Executive women confront midlife crisis. *Fortune*, 62.

68 Ibid., 68.

68 Ibid., 85.

68 This statistic was reported by Warren Farrell (1993) in *The myth of male power*. (New York: Simon & Schuster), citing research by Herbert Hildebrandt, Edwin Miller, and Dee Edington (1987). *The newly promoted executive* (monograph). Graduate School of Business Administration, University of Michigan).

74 David Schnarch (1991). *Constructing the sexual crucible: An integration of sexual and marital therapy*. (New York: W. W. Norton).

Chapter 6

75 Ventura, The age of interruption.

76 Ibid.

76 P. Aburdene and J. Naisbitt (1992). *Megatrends for women*. (New York: Villard Books), 217.

76   Ibid.

76   D. J. Swiss and J. P. Walker (1993). *Women and the work/family dilemma: How today's professional women are confronting the maternal wall.* (New York: John Wiley & Sons, Inc.).

76   Ibid.

77   Gene Landrum (1994). *Profiles of female genius—Thirteen creative women who changed the world.* (Buffalo, NY: Prometheus Books).

77   Cited in Carter and Carter, *He works/she works™.*

77   Morris, Executive women, 77.

78   Gibbs, Bring up father, 53–56.

79   David Elkind (1981). *The hurried child: Growing up too fast too soon.* (Reading, MA: Addison-Wesley), xii.

79   Ibid., 3.

80   Erkel, Time shifting, 33–39.

80   Price, *Type A behavior pattern.*

81   S. R. Sherman (May 17, 1982). The "trouble with kids" infects work. *The Boston Business Journal,* 17.

81   R. J. Burke and P. Bradshaw (1981). Occupational and life stress and the family. *Small Group Behavior,* 12(3), 329–75. Quote from p. 351.

82   Price, *Type A behavior pattern.*

82   E. Roskies (1979). Considerations in developing a treatment program for the coronary-prone (Type A) behavior pattern. In P. Davidson (Ed.), *Behavioral medicine: Changing health life styles.* (New York: Bruner/Mazel).

83   Price, *Type A behavior pattern,* 230.

83   Karen A. Matthews and Julio Angulo (1980). Measurement of the Type A behavior pattern in children: Assessment of children's competitiveness, impatience-anger, and aggression. *Child Development,* 51, 466–75.

84   Research also suggests that children who are hyperactive or suffer from attention deficit disorder are also highly likely to

be Type A. See B. D. Kennard et al. (1993). Associations of Type A behavior in children with risk factors for coronary artery disease. *Children's Health Care*, 22(4), 287–96; L. E. Stamps and C. L. Clark (1987). Relationships between the Type A behavior pattern and intelligence in children. *Journal of Genetic Psychology*, 148(4), 529–31; D. M. Murray et al. (1986). Type A behavior in children: Demographic, behavioral, and physiological correlates. *Health Psychology*, 5(2), 159–69.

84 Laurence Steinberg (1986). Stability (and instability) of Type A behavior from childhood to young adulthood. *Developmental Psychology*, 22(3), 393–402.

87 Ron Taffel (1994). *Why parents disagree: How women and men parent differently and how we can work together.* (New York: William Morrow).

Chapter 7

100 Ian Stewart and Vann Joines (1987). *TA today: A new introduction to transactional analysis.* (Nottingham: Lifespace Publishing).

Chapter 8

109 For a thorough discussion of the physiology of stress responses, see R. Eliot and D. L. Breo (1984). *Is it worth dying for?.* (New York: Bantam).

110 Janice Kiecolt-Glaser (1997). More than just a spat: Hostile arguing may compromise a woman's immune function. *Journal of Consulting and Clinical Psychology*, as reported on in *Self* (January 1997), 35.

111 For an overview of the fascinating field of study of the relationship between psychological factors and immune system

functioning (called *psychoneuroimmunology*) see R. Ornstein and D. Sobel (1987). *The healing brain: Breakthrough discoveries about how the brain keeps us healthy.* (New York: Simon & Schuster).

112   This notion (adaptation energy) is borrowed from the seminal stress researcher, Has Selye. For a more extensive discussion of Dr. Selye's research on stress, see H. Seyle (1974). *Stress without distress.* (Philadelphia: Lippincott).

112   W. M. Sotile, *Psychosocial interventions for cardiopulmonary patients.*

113   For information on the stress of life changes, and for a description of the research that led to the development of the Social Readjustment Rating Scale, see T. H. Holmes and R. H. Rahe (1968). The social readjustment rating scale. *Journal of Psychosomatic Research*, 11, 213–18.

114   Ernie Lawson. *The transformed self.* (Nightengale Motivational Tapes).

115   Elizabeth Harper-Neeld (1995). *Change awareness* (workshop manual). Baton Rouge, LA: Shell, Inc.).

120   Jack Ferner (1980). *Successful time management.* (New York: John Wiley & Sons, Inc.).

121   Sotile and Sotile, *The medical marriage.*

Chapter 9

129   Lawrence F. Van Egeren (1990). A "success trap" theory of Type A behavior: Historical background. In M. J. Strube (Ed.), Type A behavior, 45–58.

129   *Hurry sickness* is a term originated by Meyer Friedman and Ray Rosenman, researchers of Type A behavior pattern.

129   "Trading briefcases for Little League games . . . Parent track has growing appeal." As reported in *Business Life* (October, 1996), 54.

130 These strategies are our modification and elaboration of a similar list of 21 ways to reduce stress during the workday, by Saki Santorelli, as reported by Vince Bielski, Our magnificent obsession.

134 Erkel, Time shifting.

135 David Waters and J. Terry Saunders (1996). I gave at the office. *Family Therapy Networker,* 20(2), 44–51.

136 James Prochaska, John C. Norcross, and Carlo C. DiClemente (1994). *Changing for good.* (New York: William Morrow & Company).

137 Keith H. Hammonds (September 16, 1996). Balancing work and family. *Business Week,* 74–80.

137 Ibid.

139 Barnett and Rivers, *She works/he works.*

139 From Joseph Nocera. As cited by Betsy Morris (March 17, 1997). Is your family wrecking your career? *Fortune,* 74–75.

Chapter 10

149 Thanks to Vann Joines of the Southeast Institute, Chapel Hill, NC, for introducing us to this helpful exercise.

Chapter 11

161 B. F. Wilson and C. A. Schoenborn (November 1989). A healthy marriage: Does marriage foster a healthy lifestyle, or do healthy people get married? *American Demographics,* 40–43. See also J. K. Kiecolt-Glaser et al. (1987). Marital quality, marital disruption, and immune function. *Psychosomatic Medicine,* 49. 13–34; J. C. Coyne and A. DeLongis (1986). Going beyond social support: The role of social relationships in adaptation. *Journal of Consulting and Clinical Psychology,* 54(4), 454–60.

161   A. H. Yandoli (1989). Stress and medical marriages. *Stress Medicine*, 5, 213–19. See also C. S. Weisman and M. A. Teitelbaum (September 1987). The work-family role system and physician productivity. *Journal of Health and Social Behavior*, 28, 247–57.

161   W. H. Hendrix, B. A. Spencer, and G. S. Gibson (1994). Organizational and extraorganizational factors affecting stress, employee well-being, and absenteeism for males and females. *Journal of Business and Psychology*, 9(2), 103–28. See also B. Azar (1997). Quelling today's conflict between home and work. *APA Monitor*, 28(7), 1, 16.

162   R. J. Burke and T. Weir (1977). Marital helping relationships: The moderators between stress and well-being. *The Journal of Psychology*, 95, 121–30. See also S. R. Beach, E. E. Sandeen, and K. D. O'Leary (1990). *Depression in marriage*. New York: Guilford Press.

162   J. B. Schultz and C. Henderson (1985). Family satisfaction and job performance: Implications for career development. Special issue. Family-career linkages. *Journal of Career Development*, 12(1), 33–47. See also E. R. Greenglass, L. Fiksenbaum, and R. J. Burke (1994). The relationship between social support and burnout over time in teachers. *Journal of Social Behavior and Personality*, 9(2), 219–30.

162   These seven patterns were originally described in W. Sotile (1992). *Heart illness and intimacy: How caring relationships aid recovery*. (Baltimore, MD: Johns Hopkins University Press). They were further elaborated in Sotile and Sotile, *The medical marriage*, and in W. M. Sotile and M. O. Sotile (July/August 1996). High powered couples. *Psychology Today*, 50–55.

166   Harville Hendrix (1988). *Getting the love you want: A guide for couples*. (New York: Harper & Row).

170   Stewart and Joines, *TA today*.

174   Schnarch, *Constructing the sexual crucible.*

176   A 1989 study of 217 doctors and their spouses found that 43% cited work stress as contributing to significant marital discord, with 25% of the respondents indicating that they spend less than two awake hours each week dedicated to or alone with their spouses. See P. H. Fabri et al. (1989). Great expectations: Stress and the medical family. *Journal of Surgical Research*, 47(5), 379–82.

177   T. W. Smith (1992). Hostility and health: Current status of a psychosomatic hypothesis. *Health Psychology*, 11(3), 139–50.

For a discussion of the self-defeating ways that angry people create misery for themselves in interacting with others, see T. W. Smith and N. B. Anderson (1986). Models of personality and disease: An interactional approach to Type A behavior and cardiovascular risk. *Journal of Personality and Social Psychology*, 3, 1166–73; T. S. Smith and J. D. Sanders (1986). Type A behavior, marriage, and the heart: Person-by-situation interactions and the risk of coronary disease. *Behavioral Medicine Abstracts*, 7(2), 59–62.

For discussions of ways that highly hostile people create stress in relationships, see N. T. Blaney, P. Brown, and P. H. Blaney (1986). Type A, marital adjustment, and life stress. *Journal of Behavioral Medicine*, 9(5), 491–502; R. J. Burke, T. Weir, and R. E. DuWors (1979). Type A behavior of administrators and wives' reports of marital satisfaction and well-being. *Journal of Applied Psychology*, 64(1), 57–65; J. T. Condon (1988). Assessment of Type A behavior pattern: Results from a spouse-report approach. *Psychological Medicine*, 18, 747–55; D. C. Glass (1977). *Behavior patterns, stress and coronary disease*. (Hillsdale, NJ: Erlbaum); Helgeson, Status of the literature on Type A behavior; R. W. Levenson and J. M. Gottman (1983). Marital interaction: Physiological linkage and affective exchange. *Journal of Personality and Social Psychology*, 45(3), 587–97; Smith and Anderson, Models of personality and disease; Smith and Sanders, Type A behavior; J. Suls, J. W. Gastorf, and S. H. Witenberg (1979). Life events, psychological distress and the Type A coronary-prone behavior pattern. *Journal of Psychosomatic Research*, 23, 315–19; L. F. Van Egeren (1979). Social interactions, communications, and the coronary-prone behavior pattern: A psychophysiological study. *Psychosomatic Medicine*, 41, 2–18; L. F. Van Egeren, J. L. Abelson, and L. D. Sniderman (1983). Interpersonal and electrocardiographic responses of Type As and Type Bs in competitive socioeconomic games. *Journal of Psychosomatic Research*, 27, 53–59.

177   These strategies were adapted from W. M. Sotile and M. O. Sotile (1996). The angry physician: I. The temper-tantruming physician. *Physician Executive*, 22(8), 30–34, and W. M. Sotile and M. O. Sotile (1996). The angry physician: II. Managing yourself while managing others. *Physician Executive*, 22(9), 39–42.

177   From Robert Alan (1991). Anger management: A systemic program to reduce unwanted anger. (Presented at the Third National Conference of the Psychology of Health, Immunity and Disease, The National Institute for the Clinical Application of Behavioral Medicine, Orlando, FL).

177   W. M. Sotile, *Psychosocial interventions for cardiopulmonary patients*.

177   See R. Williams (1989). *The trusting heart*. (New York: Time Books).

178   R. Fisher and W. Ury (1991). *Getting to yes: Negotiating agreement without giving in*, 2nd ed. (New York: Penguin Books).

182   W. M. Sotile, *Heart illness and intimacy*, 94.

Index